**Everyman's Poetry**

*Everyman, I will go with thee,*
*and be thy guide*

# John Dryden

Selected and edited by DAVID HOPKINS
University of Bristol

EVERYMAN
J. M. Dent · London

This edition first published by Everyman Paperbacks in 1998
Selection, introduction and other critical apparatus
© J. M. Dent 1998

J. M. Dent
Orion Publishing Group
Orion House
5 Upper St Martin's Lane
London WC2H 9EA

Typeset by Deltatype Ltd, Birkenhead, Merseyside
Printed in Great Britain by
The Guernsey Press Co. Ltd, Guernsey, C. I.

British Library Cataloguing-in-Publication
Data is available on request.

ISBN 0 460 87940 5

# Contents

# Note on the Author and Editor

JOHN DRYDEN was born in Northamptonshire in 1631 and educated at Westminster School and Trinity College, Cambridge. During the 1650s he worked for the Cromwellian government, where his senior colleagues included John Milton and Andrew Marvell. After the Restoration he quickly established himself as the leading poet and literary critic of his day, most notably with *Annus Mirabilis*, an exuberant 'historical poem' celebrating the English sea-victory over the Dutch in 1666, and *Of Dramatic Poesy* (1668), a critical essay debating the relative merits of classical, French and English drama. He was soon appointed Poet Laureate (1668) and Historiographer Royal (1670). During the 1660s and 1670s his main livelihood came from his copious writing for the theatre. In the early 1680s he became involved in political and religious controversy, defending Charles II against the exclusionists in *Absalom and Achitophel* (1681) and *The Medal* (1682), and championing moderate Anglicanism in *Religio Laici* (1682). He subsequently converted to Catholicism, defending his new faith in *The Hind and the Panther* (1687). On the accession of William III in 1689, Dryden lost his court positions and returned, briefly, to the theatre. But his energies during his last years were increasingly devoted to the verse translations which, for his contemporaries, constituted the summit of his achievement. In these works he was said by William Congreve to have shown himself 'an improving writer to his last, even to near seventy years of age, improving even in fire and imagination, as well as in judgement'.

DAVID HOPKINS is Reader in English Poetry at the University of Bristol. His publications include *John Dryden* (1986), *The Routledge Anthology of Poets on Poets* (1994) and (with Tom Mason) an edition of *Abraham Cowley: Selected Poems* (1994).

# Chronology of Dryden's Life

| Year | Age | Life |
|------|-----|------|
| 1631 | | (9 August) Born at Aldwincle, Northamptonshire, to Erasmus Dryden and Mary Pickering |
| 1644 | 13 | ?Enters Westminster School |
| 1649 | 18 | *Lacrymae Musarum*, elegies on the death of Lord Hastings, with contribution by Dryden |
| 1650 | 19 | Admitted to Trinity College, Cambridge |
| 1654 | 23 | Graduates BA |
| 1657 | 26 | (October) In the employment of John Thurloe, Cromwell's Secretary of State |
| 1658 | 27 | (23 November) Walks in Cromwell's funeral procession, along with Milton and Marvell |
| 1659 | 28 | *Heroic Stanzas* published in a collection of poems on Cromwell's death |
| 1660 | 29 | (June) *Astraea Redux*, a poem celebrating the King's return |
| 1663 | 32 | (5 February) First performance of first play, *The Wild Gallant* (twenty-one other plays written in the next twenty-two years); (1 December) marries Lady Elizabeth Howard |

# Chronology of his Times

| Year | Cultural Context | Historical Events |
| --- | --- | --- |
| 1631 | Death of John Donne | |
| 1642 | Browne, *Religio Medici* | (22 August) Outbreak of First Civil War; closure of theatres |
| 1644 | Milton, *Areopagitica* | |
| 1645 | Milton, *Poems* Waller, *Poems* | (14 June) Decisive defeat of Royalists at Naseby |
| 1648 | Paris Royal Academy of Arts founded | (May–August) Second Civil War |
| 1649 | Milton, *Eikonoklastes* | (30 January) Execution of Charles I |
| 1650 | Anne Bradstreet, *Tenth Muse* | |
| 1651 | Hobbes, *Leviathan* Milton, *Pro populo Anglicano defensio* | (3 September) Prince Charles escapes after his defeat at the Battle of Worcester |
| 1653 | Walton, *Compleat Angler* | (16 December) Cromwell becomes Lord Protector |
| 1658 | Browne, *Hydrotaphia or Urn Burial* | (3 September) Death of Cromwell |
| 1660 | | (May) Restoration of Charles II; Pepys starts his *Diary* (ends 31 May 1669) |

| Year | Age | Life |
| --- | --- | --- |
| 1666 | 35 | Staying at his father-in-law's country estate at Charlton, Wiltshire, to avoid the plague; writes *Of Dramatic Poesy*; (27 August) birth of first son, Charles |
| 1667 | 36 | (January) *Annus Mirabilis*, a poem on the Dutch War and Great Fire |
| 1668 | 37 | (13 April) Appointed Poet Laureate; (spring) signs a contract with the King's Company to write three plays a year in return for a share of profits; second son, John, born |
| 1669 | 38 | (2 May) Third son, Erasmus-Henry, born |
| 1670 | 39 | (18 August) Appointed Historiographer Royal |
| 1671 | 40 | (7 December) Satirized as 'Mr Bayes' in Buckingham's *The Rehearsal*, a skit on 'heroic plays' |
| 1672 | 41 | (25 January) Theatre Royal destroyed by fire |
| 1673 | 42 | Dryden's poems and plays attacked in *The Censure of the Rota* and *The Friendly Vindication* |

| Year | Cultural Context | Historical Events |
|------|-----------------|-------------------|
| 1665 | Hooke, *Micrographia* | (February) Second Anglo-Dutch War begins (ends 1667); (June) Great Plague in London |
| 1666 | Bunyan, *Grace Abounding to the Chief of Sinners* | (2–5 September) Great Fire of London |
| 1667 | Milton, *Paradise Lost* (10-book edition) | (June) Dutch raid into the Thames estuary and Medway; (21 July) Treaty of Breda ends Dutch War; (August) fall of Clarendon and accession of the 'Cabal' |
| 1668 | Cowley, *Essays in Prose and Verse* | (January) Triple Alliance (England, Holland, Sweden) against France |
| 1670 | Pascal, *Pensées* | (22 May) Secret Treaty of Dover between Charles II and the French |
| 1671 | Milton, *Paradise Regained* and *Samson Agonistes* | |
| 1672 | | (17 March) Third Anglo-Dutch War (ends 19 February, 1674) |
| 1673 | Wren commences work on the rebuilding of St Paul's Cathedral | (29 March) Test Act excludes Catholics from office; (June) James Duke of York resigns as Lord High Admiral as a consequence; Shaftesbury begins to intrigue with Monmouth for the succession to the throne |

| Year | Age | Life |
|------|-----|------|
| 1674 | 43 | (Spring) Writes, with Milton's permission, *The State of Innocence*, an 'operatic' adaptation of *Paradise Lost* (published 1677) |
| 1675 | 44 | (Winter) Attacked in Rochester's 'An Allusion to Horace' |
| 1676 | 45 | Circulation in MS of *Mac Flecknoe*, satirizing the dramatist Thomas Shadwell |
| 1677 | 46 | |
| 1678 | 47 | |
| 1679 | 48 | Beaten up in Rose Alley by hired thugs, probably because of his supposed involvement in Mulgrave's *An Essay upon Satire* |
| 1680 | 49 | Publication by Jacob Tonson of *Ovid's Epistles*, marking Dryden's début as a translator |

| Year | Cultural Context | Historical Events |
|------|-----------------|-------------------|
| 1674 | Death of Milton<br>*Paradise Lost* (12-book edition)<br>Boileau, *L'Art Poétique* and *Le Lutrin* (both admired by Dryden) | (9 February) Treaty of Westminster, ending Anglo-Dutch war |
| 1675 | Wycherley, *The Country Wife* | |
| 1676 | Wycherley, *The Plain Dealer* | |
| 1677 | Behn, *The Rover* | (February) Shaftesbury committed to the Tower for a year after a clash with the King about the prorogation of Parliament |
| 1678 | Bunyan, *Pilgrim's Progress*, Pt. 1 | Crisis precipitated by the supposed discovery by Titus Oates and others of a Popish Plot to assassinate the King and massacre Protestants |
| 1679 | | (May) Bill brought before the Commons to exclude the Catholic Duke of York from succeeding his brother as King; (June) Charles II dissolves Parliament; James induced to go abroad, to avoid public hostility; Monmouth banished to Holland |
| 1680 | Death of Rochester | (November) Second Exclusion Bill rejected by the Lords, having passed the Commons |

| Year | Age | Life |
|------|-----|------|
| 1681 | 50 | (November) *Absalom and Achitophel*, a poem on the Popish Plot and Exclusion Crisis satirizing Shaftesbury, Buckingham and Monmouth |
| 1682 | 51 | (15/16 March) *The Medal*, a second satire on Shaftesbury, and *Religio Laici*, a poem in defence of Anglicanism |
| 1683 | 52 | |
| 1684 | 53 | (February) First volume of the Dryden/Tonson *Miscellany Poems*; (Autumn) elegy on the young poet, John Oldham |
| 1685 | 54 | (January) *Sylvae*, the second Dryden/Tonson miscellany, with important translations from Lucretius and Horace; (March) *Threnodia Augustalis* (on the death of Charles II); (November) 'To . . . Mrs Anne Killgrew' in her *Poems* (dated 1686); Dryden probably converted to Catholicism in this year |
| 1686 | 55 | |
| 1687 | 56 | (May) *The Hind and the Panther*, a defence of Roman Catholicism in beast-fable form; the poem immediately satirized by Montague and Prior in *The Hind and the Panther Transversed*; (22 November) *A Song for St Cecilia's Day* performed at the London St Cecilia 'feast' |
| 1688 | 57 | (June) *Britannia Rediviva*, celebrating the birth of the Prince |

| Year | Cultural Context | Historical Events |
| --- | --- | --- |
| 1681 | Oldham, *Satires upon the Jesuits* | Third Exclusion Bill presented to Oxford Parliament, bringing about its immediate dissolution (April); Shaftesbury imprisoned (2 July) for high treason, but acquitted (27 November) by a Whig-packed jury |
| 1682 | Otway, *Venice Preserved* | (November) Shaftesbury flees to Holland (d. 1683) |
| 1683 | | Rye House Plot to murder Charles II and the Duke of York |
| 1685 | Montaigne, *Essays*, trans. Cotton | (6 February) Death of Charles II; accession of James II; (6 July) defeat of Monmouth rebellion at Sedgemoor |
| 1686 | | Provocative pro-Catholic measures adopted by James II (continued through 1687–8) |
| 1687 | Newton, *Philosophiae naturalis principia mathematica* | |
| 1688 | Death of Bunyan Birth of Pope | (8–30 June) Trial and acquittal of the Seven Bishops for their refusal to read James II's Declaration of Indulgence (to Catholics and Dissenters); (10 June) Birth of son to James II and Queen Mary; (5 November) |

| Year | Age | Life |
|------|-----|------|
| 1689 | 58 | Loses his posts as Poet Laureate and Historiographer Royal, which are given to his old enemy Shadwell; returns to write for the theatre (five new plays to 1694) |
| 1690 | 59 | |
| 1692 | 61 | (October) Publication of *The Satires of Juvenal and Persius* (dated 1693) |
| 1693 | 62 | (July) Third Miscellany, *Examen Poeticum*, including translations from Ovid and Homer |
| 1694 | 63 | Poems to Kneller and Congreve; (15 June) signs a contract with Tonson to translate the complete works of Virgil |

| Year | Cultural Context | Historical Events |
|------|-----------------|-------------------|
| | | William of Orange lands at Torbay; (11 December) James flees London, finally escaping to France |
| 1689 | Locke, *Two Treatises of Government*<br>Locke, *Essay Concerning Human Understanding* | (6 February) William and Mary jointly offered the throne, now deemed to be 'vacant' after James's flight; James mounts expedition to Ireland, with the support of Louis XIV; (May) war declared on France (concluded, 1697) |
| 1690 | Petty, *Political Arithmetic* | (1 February) 'Non-juring' clerics deprived for refusing to take the oath of allegiance to the new monarchs; (1 July) James defeated at the Battle of the Boyne; penal laws against Catholics introduced |
| 1692 | Purcell, *The Fairy Queen* | (January) Jacobite Scots clans surrender to William III; (10 January) Duke of Malborough disgraced for corresponding secretly with James II; (13 February) Massacre of Macdonalds at Gencoe |
| 1693 | Congreve, *The Old Bachelor* | (7 April) Declaration of James II undertaking to protect the Church of England and to grant indemnity to all supporters of the Revolution, in the event of his restoration |
| 1694 | Purcell, *Te Deum* and *Jubilate* in D | (27 July) Establishment of the Bank of England; (28 December) Death of Queen Mary |

| Year | Age | Life |
| --- | --- | --- |
| 1696 | 65 | (Spring) Ode on the death of Henry Purcell (d. 21 November 1695) |
| 1697 | 66 | (July) Publication of *The Works of Virgil*; (22 November) performance of *Alexander's Feast* (with music by Jeremiah Clarke) at the St Cecilia's Day 'feast' |
| 1698 | 67 | (March) Dryden's plays attacked in Jeremy Collier's *Short View of the Immorality and Profaneness of the English Stage* |
| 1700 | 69 | (March) Publication of *Fables Ancient and Modern*, including translations from Chaucer, Ovid, Homer and Boccaccio; (1 May) Dryden's death; (2 May) buried in St Anne's Church, Soho; (13 May) reburied in Westminster Abbey; (June) publication of *The Pilgrim*, including Dryden's *Secular Masque*; Dryden lamented in *Luctus Britannici* and *The Nine Muses* (the latter consisting of poems by female admirers) |

| Year | Cultural Context | Historical Events |
|------|------------------|-------------------|
| 1696 | Vanbrugh, *The Relapse* | (March–April) Trial of Jacobites involved in the 'Fenwick' and 'Assassination' plots against William III |
| 1697 | Birth of Hogarth<br>Vanbrugh, *The Provoked Wife*<br>Congreve, *The Mourning Bride* | (21 September) Treaty of Ryswick terminates the war with France; Louis XIV recognizes William III as King of England |
| 1698 | | (11 October) First Partition Treaty with Louis XIV attempting to settle the question of the Spanish Succession on the death of King Carlos II; (14 December) Parliament votes for a massive cutback in William's standing army; William said to be contemplating abdication |
| 1700 | Congreve, *The Way of the World* | |

# Introduction

Whereas earlier English poets had been supported by patrons, or had derived their main income from sources other than their writing – whether as actors, theatre managers, diplomats, administrators, priests, tutors or persons of independent means – John Dryden was substantially dependent, for most of his life, on the proceeds of his pen. His official posts as Poet Laureate and Historiographer Royal to Charles II and James II brought him prestige and some financial rewards (though his salary from these positions was frequently in arrears), and he received occasional largess from aristocratic patrons. But his principal livelihood was derived, in his earlier years, from his writing for the theatre and, in later life, from the volumes of miscellany poems and classical translations published by his 'bookseller', Jacob Tonson. Most of Dryden's writing may be described as 'occasional' in nature, having been written in direct reponse to contemporary events and circumstances, or to meet urgent performance or publication deadlines. His plays (nearly thirty in number) followed or adapted the fashionable dramatic genres of the day, their prologues and epilogues engaging in racy banter with the Restoration theatre audience. His historical poems, verse-epistles and formal odes celebrated public events, marked ceremonial occasions and addressed friends and eminent contemporaries. His satires and discursive poems polemicized for the royal cause, pilloried literary opponents and contributed to religious controversies. His prefaces debated the latest critical issues, and defended his own writerly practices. His translations met the demands of an expanding readership, avid for accessible English renderings of the foreign classics.

The circumstances in which Dryden's poetry was written have sometimes caused him to be regarded as a writer narrowly of his time, an exclusively 'public' or 'topical' poet whose imaginative and aesthetic orientations were at one with the rationalistic ethos of Restoration England, and whose art was narrowly bounded by partisan and commercial concerns. Dryden's work, indeed, shows frequent signs of the pressures on him to flatter and propagandize, to meet urgent deadlines and to produce sorely needed box-office returns. It is, moreover, often densely allusive to current circumstances, ideas, debates and personalities. Several of his most famous poems refer closely to such contemporary events as the Second Dutch War (1665–7), the Popish Plot and Exclusion Crisis (1678–81) and the religio-political controversies leading to the Revolution of 1688–9. Others depend on equally detailed knowledge of recent theological disputes, of the Restoration theatrical world or of the life and work of contemporary dramatists, poets, antiquaries, artists, musicians and statesmen.

But Dryden's poetry is informed by far larger preoccupations and wider sympathies than might be immediately apparent from the circumstances of its production. As his earlier critics realized, Dryden's mental and imaginative 'world' was never straightforwardly coterminous with the world of events, personalities and allegiances in which he conducted his daily life. Nor were his conceptual, aesthetic or emotional perspectives limited to those provided by the culture of Restoration England. Dryden's early critics, while never underestimating the effect of local contingency on his work, depict him as a writer of wide reading, vibrant poetic energy and comprehensive imaginative vision. For these writers Dryden was a poet whose genius led him regularly, whatever the immediate task in hand, to display his true *forte*: an ability to speculate penetratingly on the larger processes of nature and to dramatize the intractable dilemmas of the human condition. 'Every page' of Dryden, wrote Samuel Johnson, 'discovers a mind very widely acquainted both with art and nature, and in full possession of great stores of intellectual wealth'. Dryden's compositions, according to Johnson, are 'the effects of a vigorous genius operating upon large materials' and constantly reveal 'the tumult of his imagination and the multitude of his ideas'. Dryden, Johnson wrote, had 'a mind very comprehensive by nature', 'peculiarly formed' for making 'penetrating remarks on human nature'. Johnson's conviction of the profundity and range of Dryden's art was fully shared by the poet's greatest nineteenth-century critic, Sir Walter Scott. 'Not only,' wrote Scott, 'did the stronger feelings of the heart, in all its dark or violent workings, but the face of natural objects, and their operation upon the human mind, pass promptly in review at his command.' The 'figures and ... landscapes' of Dryden's narratives, Scott judged, 'are presented to the mind with the same vivacity as the flow of his reasoning, or the acute metaphysical discrimination of his characters'.

The evidence of the poetry amply supports these judgements. Dryden's work, in all the genres he attempted, returns regularly to a number of large, general questions about the nature of humanity and its place in the world. How can we survive and be happy, Dryden asks, in a world controlled by powerful internal and external forces which constantly and tirelessly conspire to destroy our peace of mind? Are we merely the playthings of Fate or Fortune? Is it a source of delight or of alarm to discover that we are animated by similarly anarchic and irrational forces to those which are visible in the animal and 'inanimate' world? In what ways does human sexuality resemble that of the animals and of the immortal gods? What are the strengths and limitations of human reason? How can human beings seem so wise, yet act so foolishly? Are human societies, moral codes and systems of law 'naturally' sanctioned, or are they merely artificial constructs, permanently in conflict with our basic instincts and desires? What is the difference between wise rule and brutal tyranny? Does martial heroism show man at his most glorious or most stupid? Have women no choice but to live in a world where men make all the rules and hold all the power? Is language a well-head for truth, or a source of lies, deceptions and duplicities? Can human beings hope for an afterlife, or is death the end of all?

To summarize some of Dryden's leading preoccupations in this way is not to suggest that his 'comprehensive speculations' can be simply detached from the narrative, argumentative or topical contexts in which they are embedded, or that they form any kind of systematic theory, doctrine or manifesto. The probing questions asked by Dryden are often voiced not by the poet in his own voice, but by characters in plays or in controversial poems – or by classical or medieval writers whom Dryden is translating. And the answers provided (when any answers *are* provided) are in no way simply unanimous or univocal. Nor do they always square straight-forwardly with the opinions of Dryden the man.

From 1660 onwards Dryden was a loyal supporter of – and spokesman for – the Stuart kings. But his poetry frequently contains witty jibes at the institution of monarchy and scathing denunciations of the corruption and malice of courts. Even Dryden's most apparently partisan satires contain passages in which the opposition is presented so as to provoke amusement, fascination or wonder, rather than simply contempt. Dryden seems to have lived for much of his life as a contented family man. He loved peace and detested tyranny and militarism. But his poetry abounds in zestful depictions of violence and destruction, and his characters often voice the most vehement scorn at the sacred bonds of friendship, marriage and community. For the last fifteen years of his life Dryden was a devout Roman Catholic, but his verse of this period frequently displays conspicuous anti-clerical animus, and can on occasion articulate nihilistic sentiments and moralistic arguments with powerful conviction. Dryden's most telling imaginings of the divine, moreover, occur not in his Christian verse, but in his depictions of the amoral and licentious gods of classical antiquity. In life Dryden was known as a loyal friend, a kind counsellor, a devoted father and a good companion. In his poetry he dwelt with delighted fascination on the irrational passions, follies and crimes of humanity, as much as on its virtues and decencies. Dryden's later letters and prefaces are sometimes imbued with a melancholy and disenchanted Jacobitism. The verse of his last years is notable for its buoyant *élan* and untroubled perspicacity.

Dryden was sometimes drawn to write with an exploratory scepticism in which different points of view were set against one another in various kinds of dialogue or debate. He seems to have been able, in the act of writing, to discover and mobilize within himself imaginative sympathies of quite contradictory kinds on almost any issue, and to express them with equal eloquence and plausibility. 'When once he had engaged himself in disputation,' wrote Johnson, 'thoughts flowed in on either side: he was now no longer at a loss; he had always objections and solutions at command.' Consequently, many of his poems seem more concerned to explore the paradoxicality and complexity of problematic issues than to promote any monolithic source of wisdom or authority.

But elsewhere – sometimes for the entire duration of particular poems – Dryden could give more single-minded and whole-hearted expression to convictions and emotions apparently very different from his own. This capacity is most fully and strikingly manifested in the translations which constitute the bulk of his later verse. Translation was, for Dryden, no merely slavish or secondary activity but a 'hot fit' of creative engagement, in which he felt himself to be inhabiting the minds and souls of illustrious

predecessors – authors of radically different styles and tempera-
ments from his own – and finding a set of voices in which their
vision and poetic 'spirit' could be forcefully and vividly re-expressed
for his own times. In the act of translation Dryden was simultane-
ously reaching out to the philosophical and imaginative worlds of
'alien' writers and cultures, and activating hitherto undiscovered,
unexpressed or unrecognized parts of his own humanity and
creativity: in T. S. Eliot's words, he was 'giving the original through
himself, and finding himself through the original'. The complemen-
tary and contradictory perspectives on life which resulted from
such an activity combined to produce a body of poetry which
provides a peculiarly rich inward portrayal of the agonies and joys
of human existence. In one of his Dedications, Dryden quoted a
famous line from the Roman playwright Terence which aptly sums
up the spirit of his own work: '*homo sum, humani a me nihil alienum
puto*' ('I am a human being, and do not consider anything within
the scope of human experience to be foreign to me').

If the subject matter of Dryden's verse and the sympathies which
it displays are much broader in range and scope than has often been
ackowledged, his style, too, is more various and vivid than is
commonly recognized. His couplets seldom fall into predictable
shapes or regular formulae, but are almost endlessly varied in
movement and pace, encompassing a wide variety of *tempi* and
moods, from breakneck scurrility, through jaunty insouciance,
weary resignation, conversational ease and commanding majesty.
Dryden's verse can evoke with sensuous particularity a wide
variety of natural phenomena: the trembling expectation of a
young stallion, the stealth of a spider trapping a fly, the nervous
tremor of a hare cornered by hounds, the moist fecundity of the
earth at springtime. His vocabulary draws on a wide range of tones
and registers, from the jargon of sailors and musicians, to the idiom
of the rustic yokel and rakish gallant, and the lofty generality of the
wise philosopher. His imagery is constantly informed by a vital
awareness of the mysterious life-forces at work in the processes of
nature, from the 'green blood' which 'dances' in the 'veins' of new
grass, to the fogs 'shaken' from the 'flaggy wings' of the South
Wind, and the slow growth of a 'monarch oak', 'the patriarch of the
trees', 'rising', 'spreading' and decaying over nine centuries. The
vibrant animism which is so characteristic of Dryden's poetic

language was memorably evoked by Thomas Gray when he described how Dryden's Fancy

> Scatters from her pictured urn
> Thoughts that breathe and words that burn.

And the vigour, melody, and variety of Dryden's versification were suggested (and imitated) equally memorably by Alexander Pope, in his famous affirmation that it was Dryden who

> taught to join
> The varying verse, the full resounding line,
> The long majestic march, and energy divine.

DAVID HOPKINS

# Note on the Texts and Selection

Dryden's output is large and many of his best poems are long. For reasons suggested in the Introduction, no single poem or small group of poems can adequately represent the diversity of perspectives, sentiments, tones and imaginings which his work contains. The present selection contains a few of his shorter poems in their entirety, but consists, for the most part, of passages from longer works. These are, it is hoped, sufficiently self-contained to make an impact on their own terms, and to suggest something of the range of Dryden's imaginative interests and sympathies. Texts are based on the early (usually first) editions specified in the notes, with spelling and punctuation modernized, and paragraphing and indentation normalized. Italicized headnotes provide brief indications of the larger argumentative and narrative contexts from which the passages emanate. Endnotes gloss those words, phrases and references which are most likely to puzzle modern readers.

# John Dryden

# from **Annus Mirabilis: The Year of Wonders, 1666. An Historical Poem**

## (1)

*Prince Rupert pursues two Dutch warships.*

### 127

The warlike Prince had severed from the rest
    Two giant ships, the pride of all the main,
Which with his one so vigorously he pressed
    And flew so home they could not rise again.

### 128

Already battered, by his lee they lay,
    In vain upon the passing winds they call:     510
The passing winds through their torn canvas play,
    And flagging sails on heartless sailors fall.

### 129

Their opened sides receive a gloomy light,
    Dreadful as day let in to shades below;
Without, grim Death rides bare-faced in their sight,
    And urges entering billows as they flow.

### 130

When one dire shot, the last they could supply,
    Close by the board the Prince's mainmast bore,
All three now helpless by each other lie,
    And this offends not, and those fear no more.     520

### 131

So have I seen some fearful hare maintain
    A course, till tired before the dog she lay,
Who, stretched behind her, pants upon the plain,
    Past power to kill as she to get away:

### 132

With his lolled tongue he faintly licks his prey,
    His warm breath blows her flix up as she lies;
She, trembling, creeps upon the ground away,
    And looks back to him with beseeching eyes.


## (2)

*The Dutch fleet prepares to entrap the English.*

### 178

Now anchors weighed, the seamen shout so shrill
    That heaven and earth and the wide ocean rings;    710
A breeze from westward waits their sails to fill,
    And rests in those high beds his downy wings.

### 179

The wary Dutch this gathering storm foresaw,
    And durst not bide it on the English coast:
Behind their treacherous shallows they withdraw,
    And there lay snares to catch the British host.

### 180

So the false spider, when her nets are spread,
    Deep ambushed in her silent den does lie;
And feels far off the trembling of her thread,
    Whose filmy cord should bind the struggling fly:    720

### 181

Then, if at last she find him fast beset,
    She issues forth and runs along her loom;
She joys to touch the captive in her net,
    And drags the little wretch in triumph home.

## (3)

*The Great Fire of London breaks out at dead of night.*

### 216

The diligence of trades and noiseful gain,
  And luxury, more late, asleep were laid;
All was the night's, and in her silent reign
  No sound the rest of nature did invade.

### 217

In this deep quiet, from what source unknown,
  Those seeds of fire their fatal birth disclose;
And first, few scattering sparks about were blown,
  Big with the flames that to our ruin rose.

### 218

Then in some close-pent room it crept along,
  And smouldering as it went, in silence fed;                     870
Till th' infant monster, with devouring strong,
  Walked boldly upright with exalted head.

### 219

Now like some rich or mighty murderer
  Too great for prison, which he breaks with gold,
Who fresher for new mischiefs does appear,
  And dares the world to tax him with the old:

### 220

So scapes th' insulting fire his narrow jail,
  And makes small outlets into open air;
There the fierce winds his tender force assail,
  And beat him downward to his first repair.                      880

### 221

The winds like crafty courtesans withheld
  His flames from burning but to blow them more,
And every fresh attempt he is repelled
  With faints denials, weaker than before.

222

And now no longer letted of his prey
 He leaps up at it with enraged desire,
O'erlooks the neighbours with a wide survey,
 And nods at every house his threatening fire.


# from **Marriage A-la-Mode**


*Doralice sings of love and marriage.*


1

Why should a foolish marriage vow
 Which long ago was made,
Oblige us to each other now
 When passion is decayed?
We loved and we loved as long as we could,
 Till our love was loved out in us both:
But our marriage is dead when the pleasure is fled:
 'Twas pleasure first made it an oath.


2

If I have pleasures for a friend,
 And farther love in store,
What wrong has he whose joys did end,       10
 And who could give no more?
'Tis a madness that he should be jealous of me,
 Or that I should bar him of another:
For all we can gain is to give ourselves pain,
 When neither can hinder the other.

# from **Aureng-Zebe**

*Aureng-Zebe complains about the duplicity of life.*

When I consider life, 'tis all a cheat;
Yet, fooled with hope, men favour the deceit;
Trust on, and think tomorrow will repay:
Tomorrow's falser than the former day;
Lies worse, and while it says we shall be blessed
With some new joys, cuts off what we possessed.
Strange cozenage! None would live past years again,
Yet all hope pleasure in what yet remain;
And from the dregs of life think to receive
What the first sprightly running could not give.          10
I'm tired with waiting for this chemic gold,
Which fools us young and beggars us when old.


# from **Mac Flecknoe**

*Flecknoe determines that Shadwell should
succeed him as Monarch of Dullness.*

All human things are subject to decay,
And when Fate summons, monarchs must obey.
This Flecknoe found, who like Augustus young
Was called to empire, and had governed long;
In prose and verse was owned without dispute
Through all the realms of nonsense absolute.
This agèd prince, now flourishing in peace,
And blessed with issue of a large increase,
Worn out with business, did at length debate
To settle the succession of the state;                    10
And pondering which of all his sons was fit
To reign, and wage immortal war with wit,
Cried, ''Tis resolved; for Nature pleads that he

Should only rule who most resembles me:
Shadwell alone my perfect image bears,
Mature in dullness from his tender years;
Shadwell alone, of all my sons, is he
Who stands confirmed in full stupidity.
The rest to some faint meaning make pretence,
But Shadwell never deviates into sense.                    20
Some beams of wit on other souls may fall,
Strike through and make a lucid interval;
But Shadwell's genuine night admits no ray,
His rising fogs prevail upon the day.
Besides, his goodly fabric fills the eye,
And seems designed for thoughtless majesty:
Thoughtless as monarch oaks that shade the plain,
And, spread in solemn state, supinely reign.'

# from **Absalom and Achitophel**

## (1)

*King David and his natural son, Absalom*

In pious times, ere priestcraft did begin,
Before polygamy was made a sin,
When man on many multiplied his kind,
Ere one to one was cursedly confined;
When nature prompted, and no law denied
Promiscuous use of concubine and bride;
Then Israel's monarch, after heaven's own heart,
His vigorous warmth did variously impart
To wives and slaves: and, wide as his command,
Scattered his maker's image through the land.          10
  Michal, of royal blood, the crown did wear,
A soil ungrateful to the tiller's care;
Not so the rest, for several mothers bore
To godlike David several sons before.

But since like slaves his bed they did ascend,
No true succession could their seed attend.
    Of all this numerous progeny was none
So beautiful, so brave as Absalon:
Whether, inspired by some diviner lust,
His father got him with a greater gust,           20
Or that his conscious destiny made way
By manly beauty to imperial sway.
Early in foreign fields he won renown,
With kings and states allied to Israel's crown;
In peace the thoughts of war he could remove,
And seemed as he were only born for love.
Whate'er he did was done with so much ease,
In him alone 'twas natural to please;
His motions all accompanied with grace,
And paradise was opened in his face.           30

### (2)

*Achitophel, evil genius behind the rebellion against David*

Of these the false Achitophel was first:           150
A name to all succeeding ages cursed.
For close designs and crooked counsels fit;
Sagacious, bold, and turbulent of wit;
Restless, unfixed in principles and place,
In power unpleased, impatient of disgrace;
A fiery soul which, working out its way,
Fretted the pigmy body to decay,
And o'erinformed the tenement of clay.
A daring pilot in extremity:
Pleased with the danger, when the waves went high     160
He sought the storms; but for a calm unfit,
Would steer too nigh the sands to boast his wit.
    Great wits are sure to madness near allied,
And thin partitions do their bounds divide:
Else why should he, with wealth and honour blessed,
Refuse his age the needful hours of rest?
Punish a body which he could not please;

Bankrupt of life, yet prodigal of ease?
And all to leave what with his toil he won
To that unfeathered, two-legged thing, a son:                    170
Got while his soul did huddled notions try,
And born a shapeless lump, like anarchy.
In friendship false, implacable in hate;
Resolved to ruin or to rule the state.

## (3)

### Zimri, an unstable rebel

Some of their chiefs were princes of the land:
In the first rank of these did Zimri stand;
A man so various that he seemed to be
Not one, but all mankind's epitome;
Stiff in opinions, always in the wrong,
Was everything by starts, and nothing long;
But in the course of one revolving moon
Was chemist, fiddler, statesman, and buffoon;                    550
Then all for women, painting, rhyming, drinking,
Besides ten thousand freaks that died in thinking.
Blessed madman, who could every hour employ
With something new to wish or to enjoy!
Railing and praising were his usual themes,
And both, to show his judgement, in extremes;
So over-violent or over-civil
That every man with him was god or devil.
In squandering wealth was his peculiar art:
Nothing went unrewarded but desert.                              560
Beggared by fools whom still he found too late,
He had his jest and they had his estate.
He laughed himself from court, then sought relief
By forming parties, but could ne'er be chief;
For, spite of him, the weight of business fell
On Absalom and wise Achitophel.
Thus wicked but in will, of means bereft,
He left not faction, but of that was left.

# from **The Second Part of Absalom and Achitophel**

*Og, a drunken rebel*

Now stop your noses, readers, all and some,
For here's a tun of midnight-work to come,
Og from a treason tavern rolling home.
Round as a globe, and liquored every chink,                    460
Goodly and great he sails behind his link;
With all this bulk there's nothing lost in Og,
For every inch that is not fool is rogue:
A monstrous mass of foul corrupted matter,
As all the devils had spewed to make the batter.
When wine has giv'n him courage to blaspheme,
He curses God, but God before cursed him;
And if man could have reason, none has more
That made his paunch so rich, and him so poor.
With wealth he was not trusted, for heaven knew             470
What 'twas of old to pamper up a Jew;
To what would he on quail and pheasant swell,
That ev'n on tripe and carrion could rebel?
But though heav'n made him poor (with rev'rence speaking)
He never was a poet of God's making.
The midwife laid her hand on his thick skull
With this prophetic blessing: 'Be thou dull!'
Drink, swear and roar, forbear no lewd delight
Fit for thy bulk; do anything but write:
Thou art of lasting make like thoughtless men,               480
A strong nativity – but for the pen;
Eat opium, mingle arsenic in thy drink,
Still thou may'st live avoiding pen and ink.
I see, I see 'tis counsel giv'n in vain,
For treason botched in rhyme will be thy bane;
Rhyme is the rock on which thou art to wreck,
'Tis fatal to thy fame and to thy neck: . . .
To die for faction is a common evil,

But to be hanged for nonsense is the devil:
Hadst thou the glories of thy king expressed,                    500
Thy praises had been satire at the best;
But thou in clumsy verse, unlicked, unpointed,
Hast shamefully defied the Lord's anointed:
I will not rake the dunghill of thy crimes,
For who would read thy life that reads thy rhymes?


# from Religio Laici, or A Layman's Faith


## (1)

### *The limits of reason*

Dim as the borrowed beams of moon and stars
To lonely, weary, wandering travellers
Is reason to the soul; and as on high
Those rolling fires discover but the sky,
Not light us here, so reason's glimmering ray
Was lent, not to assure our doubtful way,
But guide us upward to a better day;
And as those nightly tapers disappear
When day's bright lord ascends our hemisphere,
So pale grows reason at religion's sight,                    10
So dies, and so dissolves in supernatural light.
    Some few whose lamp shone brighter have been led
From cause to cause, to nature's secret head,
And found that one first principle must be:
But what, or who, that universal he –
Whether some soul encompassing this ball,
Unmade, unmoved, yet making, moving all;
Or various atoms' interfering dance
Leaped into form, the noble work of chance,
Or this great all was from eternity –                    20
Not ev'n the Stagyrite himself could see,
And Epicurus guessed as well as he.

As blindly groped they for a future state,
As rashly judged of providence and fate.
But least of all could their endeavours find
What most concerned the good of human kind:
For happiness was never to be found,
But vanished from 'em like enchanted ground.
   One thought content the good to be enjoyed;
This every little accident destroyed. 30
The wiser madmen did for virtue toil,
A thorny, or at best a barren soil.
In pleasure some their glutton souls would steep,
But found their line too short, the well too deep,
And leaky vessels which no bliss could keep.
Thus anxious thoughts in endless circles roll,
Without a centre where to fix the soul:
In this wild maze their vain endeavours end;
How can the less the greater comprehend?
Or finite reason reach infinity? 40
For what could fathom God were more than he.


## To the Memory of Mr Oldham


Farewell, too little and too lately known,
Whom I began to think and call my own:
For sure our souls were near allied, and thine
Cast in the same poetic mould with mine.
One common note on either lyre did strike,
And knaves and fools we both abhorred alike:
To the same goal did both our studies drive;
The last set out, the soonest did arrive.
Thus Nisus fell upon the slippery place,
Whilst his young friend performed and won the race. 10
O early ripe! to thy abundant store
What could advancing age have added more?
It might (what Nature never gives the young)
Have taught the numbers of thy native tongue;

But satire needs not those, and wit will shine
Through the harsh cadence of a rugged line:
A noble error, and but seldom made,
When poets are by too much force betrayed.
Thy generous fruits, though gathered ere their prime,
Still showed a quickness; and maturing time　　　　20
But mellows what we write to the dull sweets of rhyme.
Once more, hail and farewell; farewell, thou young
But ah, too short Marcellus of our tongue!
Thy brows with ivy and with laurels bound;
But fate and gloomy night encompass thee around.

# from Sylvae, or The Second Part of Poetical Miscellanies

## from Lucretius: The Beginning of the First Book

*Lucretius hymns the universal power of Venus.*

Delight of human kind and gods above,
Parent of Rome, propitious Queen of Love,
Whose vital power air, earth and sea supplies,
And breeds whate'er is born beneath the rolling skies;
For every kind, by thy prolific might,
Springs, and beholds the regions of the light.
Thee, goddess, thee the clouds and tempests fear,
And at thy pleasing presence disappear;
For thee the land in fragrant flowers is dressed;
For thee the ocean smiles, and smooths her wavy breast,          10
And heaven itself with more serene and purer light is blessed.
    For when the rising spring adorns the mead,
And a new scene of nature stands displayed,
When teeming buds and cheerful greens appear,
And western gales unlock the lazy year;
The joyous birds thy welcome first express,
Whose native songs thy genial fire confess;
Then savage beasts bound o'er their slighted food,
Struck with thy darts, and tempt the raging flood:
All nature is thy gift, earth, air and sea,          20
Of all that breathes the various progeny,
Stung with delight, is goaded on by thee.
O'er barren mountains, o'er the flowery plain,
The leafy forest and the liquid main
Extends thy uncontrolled and boundless reign;
Through all the living regions dost thou move,
And scatter'st where thou goest the kindly seeds of love.

# from Translation of the Latter Part of the Third Book of Lucretius: Against the Fear of Death

## (1)

### *Death, the end of all*

What has this bugbear death to frighten man,
If souls can die, as well as bodies can?
For, as before our birth we felt no pain,
When Punic arms infested land and main,
When heaven and earth were in confusion hurled
For the debated empire of the world,
Which awed with dreadful expectation lay,
Sure to be slaves, uncertain who should sway:
So, when our mortal frame shall be disjoined,
The lifeless lump uncoupled from the mind,    10
From sense of grief and pain we shall be free;
We shall not feel, because we shall not *be*.
Though earth in seas, and seas in heaven were lost,
We should not move, we only should be tossed.
    Nay, ev'n suppose when we have suffered fate,.
The soul could feel in her divided state,
What's that to us? for we are only we
While souls and bodies in one frame agree.
Nay, though our atoms should revolve by chance,
And matter leap into the former dance;    20
Though time our life and motion could restore,
And make our bodies what they were before,
What gain to us would all this bustle bring?
The new-made man would be another thing;
When once an interrupting pause is made,
That individual being is decayed.
We, who are dead and gone, shall bear no part
In all the pleasures, nor shall feel the smart,
Which to that other mortal shall accrue,
Whom of our matter time shall mould anew.    30
    For backward if you look on that long space

Of ages past, and view the changing face
Of matter, tossed and variously combined
In sundry shapes, 'tis easy for the mind
From thence t' infer that seeds of things have been
In the same order as they now are seen;
Which yet our dark remembrance cannot trace,
Because a pause of life, a gaping space
Has come betwixt, where memory lies dead,
And all the wandering motions from the sense are fled.          40
For whoso'er shall in misfortunes live,
Must *be* when those misfortunes shall arrive;
And since the man who *is* not, feels not woe
(For death exempts him, and wards off the blow,
Which we the living only feel and bear),
What is there left for us in death to fear?
When once that pause of life has come between,
'Tis just the same as we had never been.

## (2)

*Nature rebukes man for squandering her gifts.*

And last, suppose great Nature's voice should call
To thee, or me, or any of us all,
'What dost thou mean, ungrateful wretch, thou vain,
Thou mortal thing, thus idly to complain,
And sigh and sob that thou shalt be no more?
For if thy life were pleasant heretofore,
If all the bounteous blessings I could give
Thou hast enjoyed, if thou hast known to live,
And pleasure not leaked through thee like a sieve,
Why dost thou not give thanks as at a plenteous feast,          130
Crammed to the throat with life, and rise and take thy rest?
     But if my blessings thou hast thrown away,
If indigested joys passed through and would not stay,
Why dost thou wish for more to squander still?
If life be grown a load, a real ill,
And I would all thy cares and labours end,
Lay down thy burden, fool, and know thy friend.

To please thee I have emptied all my store;
I can invent and can supply no more,
But run the round again, the round I ran before.                    140
Suppose thou art not broken yet with years,
Yet still the self-same scene of things appears,
And would be ever, could'st thou ever live;
For life is still but life, there's nothing new to give.'
    What can we plead against so just a bill?
We stand convicted, and our cause goes ill.
But if a wretch, a man oppressed by fate,
Should beg of Nature to prolong his date,
She speaks aloud to him with more disdain,
'Be still, thou martyr fool, thou covetous of pain!'               150
But if an old decrepit sot lament,
'What, thou', she cries, 'who hast outlived content!
Dost thou complain, who hast enjoyed my store?
But this is still th' effect of wishing more.
Unsatisfied with all that Nature brings,
Loathing the present, liking absent things;
From hence it comes thy vain desires, at strife
Within themselves, have tantalized thy life,
And ghastly death appeared before thy sight
Ere thou had'st gorged thy soul and senses with delight.            160
Now leave those joys unsuiting to thy age
To a fresh comer, and resign the stage.'
    Is Nature to be blamed if thus she chide?
No, sure; for 'tis her business to provide
Against this ever-changing frame's decay,
New things to come, and old to pass away.
One being worn, another being makes;
Changed but not lost; for Nature gives and takes:
New matter must be found for things to come,
And these must waste like those, and follow Nature's doom.          170
All things, like thee, have time to rise and rot,
And from each other's ruin are begot:
For life is not confined to him or thee;
'Tis given to all for use, to none for property.

## (3)

*Mythological torments to be found in this world, not in Hades*

Consider former ages past and gone,
Whose circles ended long ere thine begun,
Then tell me fool, what part in them thou hast?
Thus may'st thou judge the future by the past.
What horror seest thou in that quiet state,
What bugbear dreams to fright thee after fate?                      180
No ghost, no goblins that still passage keep,
But all is there serene in that eternal sleep.
For all the dismal tales that poets tell
Are verified on earth, and not in hell.
No Tantalus looks up with fearful eye,
Or dreads th' impending rock to crush him from on high:
But fear of chance on earth disturbs our easy hours,
Or vain imagined wrath, of vain imagined powers.
No Tityus torn by vultures lies in hell,
Nor could the lobes of his rank liver swell                        190
To that prodigious mass for their eternal meal;
Not though his monstrous bulk had covered o'er
Nine spreading acres, or nine thousand more;
Not though the globe of earth had been the giant's floor;
Nor in eternal torments could he lie,
Nor could his corpse sufficient food supply.
       But he's the Tityus, who by love oppressed,
Or tyrant passion preying on his breast,
And ever-anxious thoughts is robbed of rest.
The Sisyphus is he, whom noise and strife                          200
Seduce from all the soft retreats of life,
To vex the government, disturb the laws,
Drunk with the fumes of popular applause;
He courts the giddy crowd to make him great,
And sweats and toils in vain to mount the sovereign seat.
For still to aim at power, and still to fail,

Ever to strive, and never to prevail,
What is it, but in reason's true account
To heave the stone against the rising mount;
Which urged, and laboured, and forced up with pain,    210
Recoils, and rolls impetuous down, and smokes along the
    plain?


## (4)

### *Studying Nature's laws*

O, if the foolish race of man, who find
A weight of cares still pressing on their mind,
Could find as well the cause of this unrest,
And all this burden lodged within the breast,
Sure they would change their course, nor live as now,
Uncertain what to wish or what to vow.
Uneasy both in country and in town,
They search a place to lay their burden down.
One restless in his palace walks abroad,
And vainly thinks to leave behind the load;    280
But straight returns, for he's as restless there,
And finds there's no relief in open air.
Another to his villa would retire,
And spurs as hard as if it were on fire;
No sooner entered at his country door,
But he begins to stretch, and yawn, and snore,
Or seeks the city which he left before.
    Thus every man o'erworks his weary will,
To shun himself and to shake off his ill;
The shaking fit returns and hangs upon him still.    290
No prospect of repose nor hope of ease,
The wretch is ignorant of his disease;
Which known would all his fruitless trouble spare,
For he would know the world not worth his care:
Then would he search more deeply for the cause,
And study nature well, and nature's laws:
For in this moment lies not the debate,
But on our future, fixed, eternal state;

That never-changing state which all must keep,
Whom death has doomed to everlasting sleep.                    300

## from Lucretius: The Fourth Book, Concerning the Nature of Love

*Lucretius depicts the torments of love.*

When love its utmost vigour does employ,
Ev'n then 'tis but a restless wandering joy;
Nor knows the lover in that wild excess,
With hands or eyes, what first he would possess,
But strains at all, and fastening where he strains,
Too closely presses with his frantic pains;                   40
With biting kisses hurts the twining fair,
Which shows his joys imperfect, unsincere:
For stung with inward rage he flings around,
And strives t' avenge the smart on that which gave the wound.
    But love those eager bitings does restrain,
And mingling pleasure mollifies the pain.
For ardent hope still flatters anxious grief,
And sends him to his foe to seek relief:
Which yet the nature of the thing denies;
For love, and love alone of all our joys,                     50
By full possession does but fan the fire;
The more we still enjoy, the more we still desire.
Nature for meat and drink provides a space,
And when received they fill their certain place;
Hence thirst and hunger may be satisfied,
But this repletion is to love denied:
Form, feature, colour, whatsoe'er delight
Provokes the lover's endless appetite,
These fill no space, nor can we thence remove
With lips, or hands, or all our instruments of love:          60
In our deluded grasp we nothing find

But thin aërial shapes that fleet before the mind.
As he who in a dream with drought is cursed,
And finds no real drink to quench his thirst,
Runs to imagined lakes his heat to steep,
And vainly swills and labours in his sleep;
So love with phantoms cheats our longing eyes,
Which hourly seeing never satisfies;
Our hands pull nothing from the parts they strain,
But wander o'er the lovely limbs in vain.                    70
    Nor when the youthful pair more closely join,
When hands in hands they lock, and thighs in thighs they
   twine,
Just in the raging foam of full desire,
When both press on, both murmur, both expire,
They gripe, they squeeze, their humid tongues they dart,
As each would force their way to t'other's heart –
In vain; they only cruise about the coast,
For bodies cannot pierce, nor be in bodies lost,
As sure they strive to be, when both engage
In that tumultuous momentany rage;                          80
So tangled in the nets of love they lie,
Till man dissolves in that excess of joy.
Then, when the gathered bag has burst its way,
And ebbing tides the slackened nerves betray,
A pause ensues; and nature nods awhile,
Till with recruited rage new spirits boil;
And then the same vain violence returns,
With flames renewed th' erected furnace burns;
Again they in each other would be lost,
But still by adamantine bars are crossed.                   90
All ways they try, successless all they prove,
To cure the secret sore of lingering love.

# Horace: Book 1, Ode 9

### 1

Behold yon mountain's hoary height,
    Made higher with new mounts of snow;
Again behold the winter's weight
    Oppress the labouring woods below;
And streams with icy fetters bound,
Benumbed and cramped to solid ground.

### 2

With well-heaped logs dissolve the cold,
    And feed the genial hearth with fires;
Produce the wine that makes us bold,
    And sprightly wit and love inspires:        10
For what hereafter shall betide,
God, if 'tis worth his care, provide.

### 3

Let him alone with what he made,
    To toss and turn the world below;
At his command the storms invade,
    The winds by his commission blow;
Till with a nod he bids 'em cease,
And then the calm returns, and all is peace.

### 4

Tomorrow and her works defy,
    Lay hold upon the present hour,        20
And snatch the pleasures passing by,
    To put them out of Fortune's power:
Nor love, nor love's delights, disdain;
Whate'er thou get'st today is gain.

### 5

Secure those golden early joys,
    That youth unsoured with sorrow bears,
Ere withering time the taste destroys,
    With sickness and unwieldy years.

For active sports, for pleasing rest,
This is the time to be possessed;                                    30
The best is but in season best.


6

The pointed hour of promised bliss,
    The pleasing whisper in the dark,
The half-unwilling willing kiss,
    The laugh that guides thee to the mark,
When the kind nymph would coyness feign,
And hides but to be found again:
These, these are joys the gods for youth ordain.


# Horace: Book 3, Ode 29, Paraphrased in Pindaric Verse, and Inscribed to the Right Honourable Lawrence, Earl of Rochester


1

Descended of an ancient line
That long the Tuscan sceptre swayed,
Make haste to meet the generous wine
Whose piercing is for thee delayed:
The rosy wreath is ready made,
    And artful hands prepare
The fragrant Syrian oil that shall perfume thy hair.


2

When the wine sparkles from afar,
And the well-natured friend cries, 'Come away!'
Make haste, and leave thy business and thy care;     10
No mortal interest can be worth thy stay.


3

Leave for a while thy costly country seat,
    And, to be great indeed, forget

The nauseous pleasures of the great:
    Make haste and come;
Come, and forsake thy cloying store,
Thy turret that surveys from high
The smoke, and wealth and noise of Rome,
And all the busy pageantry
That wise men scorn, and fools adore;                    20
Come, give thy soul a loose, and taste the pleasures of the
poor.


4

Sometimes 'tis grateful to the rich to try
A short vicissitude, and fit of poverty:
    A savoury dish, a homely treat,
    Where all is plain, where all is neat,
    Without the stately spacious room,
The Persian carpet or the Tyrian loom,
Clear up the cloudy foreheads of the great.


5

The sun is in the lion mounted high;
      The Sirian star                    30
      Barks from afar,
And with his sultry breath infects the sky;
The ground below is parched, the heavens above us fry:
    The shepherd drives his fainting flock
    Beneath the covert of a rock,
    And seeks refreshing rivulets nigh:
The sylvans to their shades retire,
Those very shades and streams new shades and streams
    require,
And want a cooling breeze of wind to fan the raging fire.


6

Thou, what befits the new Lord Mayor,                    40
And what the City faction dare,
And what the Gallic arms will do,
And what the quiver-bearing foe,
Art anxiously inquisitive to know;
But God has wisely hid from human sight

The dark decrees of future fate,
And sown their seeds in depth of night;
He laughs at all the giddy turns of state,
When mortals search too soon, and fear too late.

7

Enjoy the present smiling hour,                    50
And put it out of Fortune's power;
The tide of business, like the running stream,
Is sometimes high and sometimes low,
A quiet ebb or a tempestuous flow,
And always in extreme.
Now with a noiseless gentle course
It keeps within the middle bed;
Anon it lifts aloft the head,
And bears down all before it with impetuous force:
And trunks of trees come rolling down,             60
Sheep and their folds together drown;
Both house and homestead into seas are borne,
And rocks are from their old foundations torn,
And woods made thin with winds their scattered honours
   mourn.

8

Happy the man, and happy he alone,
He who can call today his own:
He who secure within can say,
'Tomorrow do thy worst, for I have lived today:
Be fair, or foul, or rain, or shine,
The joys I have possessed, in spite of Fate, are mine;  70
Not heaven itself upon the past has power,
But what has been has been, and I have had my hour.'

9

Fortune, that with malicious joy
Does man her slave oppress,
Proud of her office to destroy,
Is seldom pleased to bless;
Still various, and unconstant still,
But with an inclination to be ill,

Promotes, degrades, delights in strife,
And makes a lottery of life. 80
I can enjoy her while she's kind;
But when she dances in the wind,
And shakes her wings and will not stay,
I puff the prostitute away:
The little or the much she gave is quietly resigned;
Content with poverty, my soul I arm,
And virtue, though in rags, will keep me warm.

10
What is't to me,
Who never sail in her unfaithful sea,
If storms arise, and clouds grow black; 90
If the mast split, and threaten wrack?
Then let the greedy merchant fear
For his ill-gotten gain;
And pray to gods that will not hear,
While the debating winds and billows bear
His wealth into the main.
For me, secure from Fortune's blows
(Secure of what I cannot lose),
In my small pinnace I can sail,
Contemning all the blustering roar, 100
And running with a merry gale,
With friendly stars my safety seek
Within some little winding creek,
And see the storm ashore.

# A New Song

1
Sylvia the fair, in the bloom of fifteen,
Felt an innocent warmth as she lay on the green;
She had heard of a pleasure, and something she guessed
By the tousing and tumbling and touching her breast.

She saw the men eager, but was at a loss
What they meant by their sighing and kissing so close:
　　By their praying and whining,
　　And clasping and twining,
　　And panting and wishing,
　　And sighing and kissing,　　　　　　　　　　　10
　　And sighing and kissing so close.

2

'Ah', she cried, 'ah, for a languishing maid,
In a country of Christians to die without aid!
Not a Whig or a Tory, or Trimmer at least,
Or a Protestant parson or Catholic priest,
To instruct a young virgin that is at a loss
What they meant by their sighing and kissing so close!
　　By their praying and whining,
　　And clasping and twining,
　　And panting and wishing,　　　　　　　　　　　20
　　And sighing and kissing,
　　And sighing and kissing so close.'

3

Cupid in shape of a swain did appear,
He saw the sad wound and in pity drew near;
Then showed her his arrow and bid her not fear,
For the pain was no more than a maiden may bear.
When the balm was infused, she was not at a loss
What they meant by their sighing and kissing so close:
　　By their praying and whining,
　　And clasping and twining,　　　　　　　　　　　30
　　And panting and wishing,
　　And sighing and kissing,
　　And sighing and kissing so close.

# from To the Pious Memory of the Accomplished Young Lady, Mrs Anne Killigrew, Excellent in the Two Sister-Arts of Poesy and Painting: An Ode

Thou youngest virgin-daughter of the skies,
Made in the last promotion of the blessed,
Whose palms, new plucked from paradise,
In spreading branches more sublimely rise,
Rich with immortal green above the rest:
Whether, adopted to some neighbouring star,
Thou roll'st above us in thy wandering race,
Or, in procession fixed and regular,
    Moved with the heavens' majestic pace;
    Or, called to more superior bliss,         10
Thou tread'st with seraphims the vast abyss:
Whatever happy region is thy place,
Cease thy celestial song a little space
(Thou wilt have time enough for hymns divine,
    Since heaven's eternal year is thine).
Hear, then, a mortal Muse thy praise rehearse,
    In no ignoble verse;
But such as thy own voice did practise here,
When thy first fruits of poesy were given,
To make thyself a welcome inmate there;       20
    While yet a young probationer,
    And candidate of heaven.

# from **The Hind and the Panther, Part 1**

*The origins of tyranny and persecution*

Of all the tyrannies on human kind
The worst is that which persecutes the mind.                240
Let us but weigh at what offence we strike;
'Tis but because we cannot think alike.
In punishing of this, we overthrow
The laws of nations and of nature too.
Beasts are the subjects of tyrannic sway,
Where still the stronger on the weaker prey;
Man only of a softer mould is made,
Not for his fellows' ruin, but their aid;
Created kind, beneficent and free,
The noble image of the Deity.                               250
    One portion of informing fire was given
To brutes, th' inferior family of heaven.
The smith divine, as with a careless beat,
Struck out the mute creation at a heat;
But, when arrived at last to human race,
The godhead took a deep considering space;
And, to distinguish man from all the rest,
Unlocked the sacred treasures of his breast;
And mercy, mixed with reason, did impart,
One to his head, the other to his heart;                    260
Reason to rule, but mercy to forgive;
The first is law, the last prerogative.
And like his mind his outward form appeared,
When, issuing naked to the wondering herd,
He charmed their eyes; and for they loved, they feared.
Not armed with horns of arbitrary might,
Or claws to seize their furry spoils in fight,
Or with increase of feet t' o'ertake them in their flight;
Of easy shape, and pliant every way,
Confessing still the softness of his clay,                  270
And kind as kings upon their coronation day;
With open hands, and with extended space
Of arms, to satisfy a large embrace.

Thus kneaded up with milk, the new-made man
His kingdom o'er his kindred world began;
Till knowledge misapplied, misunderstood,
And pride of empire soured his balmy blood.
Then first rebelling his own stamp he coins;
The murd'rer Cain was latent in his loins;
And blood began its first and loudest cry,                      280
For differing worship of the Deity.
Thus persecution rose, and farther space
Produced the mighty hunter of his race.


# A Song for St Cecilia's Day, 1687


### 1

From harmony, from heavenly harmony,
  This universal frame began:
  When Nature underneath a heap
   Of jarring atoms lay,
   And could not heave her head,
  The tuneful voice was heard from high,
   'Arise, ye more than dead!'
  Then cold and hot and moist and dry
  In order to their stations leap,
   And music's power obey.                              10
From harmony, from heavenly harmony,
  This universal frame began:
  From harmony to harmony
Through all the compass of the notes it ran,
The diapason closing full in man.


### 2

  What passion cannot music raise and quell?
  When Jubal struck and chorded shell,
  His listening brethren stood around,
  And wondering on their faces fell
  To worship that celestial sound.                         20

Less than a god they thought there could not dwell
    Within the hollow of that shell,
    That spoke so sweetly and so well.
What passion cannot music raise and quell?

3

    The trumpet's loud clangour
      Excites us to arms,
    With shrill notes of anger
      And mortal alarms.
The double, double, double beat
      Of the thundering drum                        30
Cries, 'Hark! the foes come;
Charge, charge, 'tis too late to retreat!'

4

    The soft complaining flute
    In dying notes discovers
    The woes of hopeless lovers,
Whose dirge is whispered by the warbling lute.

5

    Sharp violins proclaim
Their jealous pangs and desperation,
    Fury, frantic indignation,
    Depth of pains, and height of passion          40
    For the fair, disdainful dame.

6

    But oh! what art can teach,
    What human voice can reach
    The sacred organ's praise?
Notes inspiring holy love,
Notes that wing their heavenly ways
    To mend the choirs above.

7

Orpheus could lead the savage race,
And trees unrooted left their place,
    Sequacious of the lyre:                        50

But bright Cecilia raised the wonder higher:
When to her organ vocal breath was given
    An angel heard, and straight appeared,
      Mistaking earth for heaven.

       *GRAND CHORUS*
*As from the power of sacred lays*
    *The spheres began to move,*
*And sung the great Creator's praise*
    *To all the blessed above;*
*So when the last and dreadful hour*
*This crumbling pageant shall devour,*       60
*The trumpet shall be heard on high,*
*The dead shall live, the living die,*
*And music shall untune the sky.*


# from **Eleonora: A Panegyrical Poem**


*The death of Eleonora, Countess of Abingdon*

She vanished, we can scarcely say she died;
For but a now did heaven and earth divide:
She passed serenely with a single breath;
This moment perfect health, the next was death:
One sigh did her eternal bliss assure;
So little penance needs, when souls are almost pure.     310
As gentle dreams our waking thoughts pursue,
Or, one dream passed, we slide into a new;
So close they follow, such wild order keep,
We think ourselves awake, and are asleep;
So softly death succeeded life in her,
She did but dream of heaven and she was there.

# from **The Satires of Juvenal and Persius**

## from **The Sixth Satire of Juvenal**

*The nocturnal activities of Messalina, wife of the Emperor Claudius*

The good old sluggard but began to snore,
When from his side up rose th' imperial whore;
She who preferred the pleasures of the night
To pomps, that are but impotent delight,
Strode from the palace with an eager pace,
To cope with a more masculine embrace.
Muffled she marched, like Juno in a cloud,
Of all her train but one poor wench allowed;        170
One whom in secret service she could trust:
The rival and companion of her lust.
To the known brothel-house she takes her way,
And for a nasty room gives double pay;
That room in which the rankest harlot lay.
Prepared for fight, expectingly she lies,
With heaving breasts and with desiring eyes.
Still as one drops, another takes his place,
And baffled still succeeds to like disgrace.
At length, when friendly darkness is expired,        180
And every strumpet from her cell retired,
She lags behind and, lingering at the gate,
With a repining sigh submits to fate;
All filth without, and all afire within,
Tired with the toil, unsated with the sin.
Old Caesar's bed the modest matron seeks,
The steam of lamps still hanging on her cheeks
In ropy smut; thus foul, and thus bedight,
She brings him back the product of the night.

# from **The Tenth Satire of Juvenal**

## (1)

*The fall of Sejanus, favourite of the Emperor Tiberius*

Some ask for envied power, which public hate
Pursues, and hurries headlong to their fate:
Down go the titles, and the statue crowned
Is by base hands in the next river drowned.
The guiltless horses and the chariot wheel
The same effects of vulgar fury feel:                          90
The smith prepares his hammer for the stroke,
While the lunged bellows hissing fire provoke.
Sejanus, almost first of Roman names,
The great Sejanus crackles in the flames:
Formed in the forge, the pliant brass is laid
On anvils; and of head and limbs are made
Pans, cans and piss-pots, a whole kitchen trade.
      Adorn your doors with laurels, and a bull,
Milk white and large, lead to the Capitol;
Sejanus with a rope is dragged along.                          100
The sport and laughter of the giddy throng.
      'Good lord,' they cry, 'what Ethiop lips he has;
How foul a snout, and what a hanging face!
By heaven, I never could endure his sight!
But say, how came his monstrous crimes to light?
What is the charge, and who the evidence?
The saviour of the nation and the prince?'
'Nothing of this, but our old Caesar sent
A noisy letter to his parliament.'
'Nay, sirs, if Caesar writ, I ask no more;                     110
He's guilty, and the question's out of door.'
How goes the mob (for that's a mighty thing)?
When the king's trump, the mob are for the king;
They follow fortune, and the common cry
Is still against the rogue condemned to die.
      But the same very mob, that rascal crowd,
Had cried 'Sejanus' with a shout as loud,

Had his designs, by Fortune's favour blessed,
Succeeded, and the prince's age oppressed.
But long, long since the times have changed their face,          120
The people grown degenerate and base;
Not suffered now the freedom of their choice
To make their magistrates and sell their voice.
    Our wise forefathers, great by sea and land,
Had once the power and absolute command,
All offices of trust themselves disposed,
Raised whom they pleased, and whom they pleased deposed:
But we who give our native rights away,
And our enslaved posterity betray,
Are now reduced to beg an alms, and go          130
On holidays to see a puppet show.
    'There was a damned design,' cries one, 'no doubt,
For warrants are already issued out:
I met Brutidius in a mortal fright,
He's dipped for certain, and plays least in sight;
I fear the rage of our offended prince,
Who thinks the Senate slack in his defence.
Come, let us haste our loyal zeal to show,
And spurn the wretched corpse of Caesar's foe:
But let our slaves be present there, lest they          140
Accuse their masters and for gain betray.'
    Such were the whispers of those jealous times
About Sejanus' punishment and crimes.
    Now tell me truly, wouldst thou change thy fate,
To be, like him, first minister of state?
To have thy levees crowded with resort
Of a depending, gaping, servile court;
Dispose all honours of the sword and gown,
Grace with a nod and ruin with a frown;
To hold thy prince in pupillage and sway:          150
That monarch whom the mastered world obey;
While he, intent on secret lusts alone,
Lives to himself, abandoning the throne;
Cooped in a narrow isle, observing dreams
With flattering wizards, and erecting schemes?
    I well believe thou wouldst be great as he,
For every man's a fool to that degree:

All wish the dire prerogative to kill;
Ev'n they would have the power who want the will:
But wouldst thou have thy wishes understood,                160
To take the bad together with the good?
Wouldst thou not rather choose a small renown,
To be the mayor of some poor paltry town;
Bigly to look and barb'rously to speak;
To pound false weights and scanty measures break?
Then, grant we that Sejanus went astray
In every wish, and knew not how to pray;
For he who grasped the world's exhausted store,
Yet never had enough, but wished for more,
Raised a top-heavy tower of monstrous height,                170
Which, mouldering, crushed him underneath the weight.


## (2)

### *The miseries of old age*

'Jove, grant me length of life, and years' good store
Heap on my bending back: I ask no more.'
Both sick and healthful, old and young, conspire
In this one silly, mischievous desire.
Mistaken blessing which old age they call:
'Tis a long, nasty, darksome hospital;
A ropy chain of rheums, a visage rough,
Deformed, unfeatured, and a skin of buff;
A stitch-fall'n cheek that hangs below the jaw;
Such wrinkles as a skilful hand would draw                310
For an old grandam ape, when, with a grace,
She sits at squat and scrubs her leathern face.
        In youth, distinctions infinite abound;
No shape or feature just alike are found:
The fair, the black, the feeble, and the strong.
But the same foulness does to age belong,
The self-same palsy both in limbs and tongue;
The skull and forehead one bald barren plain,
And gums unarmed to mumble meat in vain;
Besides th' eternal drivel that supplies                320

The dropping beard from nostrils, mouth, and eyes.
His wife and children loathe him, and, what's worse,
Himself does his offensive carrion curse!
Flatt'rers forsake him too; for who would kill
Himself to be remembered in a will?
His taste not only palled to wine and meat,
But to the relish of a nobler treat.
The limber nerve, in vain provoked to rise,
Inglorious from the field of battle flies;
Poor feeble dotard, how could he advance                    330
With his blue headpiece and his broken lance?
Add that, endeavouring still without effect,
A lust more sordid justly we suspect.

# from **To my Dear Friend, Mr Congreve, on his Comedy called *The Double Dealer***

*Dryden hails Congreve as his poetic heir.*

O, that your brows my laurel had sustained:
Well had I been deposed if you had reigned!
The father had descended for the son;
For only you are lineal to the throne.
Thus, when the state one Edward did depose,
A greater Edward in his room arose.
But now not I, but poetry is cursed;
For Tom the second reigns like Tom the first.
But let 'em not mistake my patron's part,
Nor call his charity their own desert.                      50
Yet this I prophesy: thou shalt be seen
(Though with some short parenthesis between)
High on the throne of wit, and, seated there,
Not mine – that's little – but thy laurel wear.
Thy first attempt an early promise made;
That early promise this has more than paid.
So bold yet so judiciously you dare,
That your least praise is to be regular.

Time, place and action may with pains be wrought,
But genius must be born, and never can be taught.          60
This is your portion, this your native store;
Heaven, that but once was prodigal before,
To Shakespeare gave as much; she could not give him more.
    Maintain your post: that's all the fame you need;
For 'tis impossible you should proceed.
Already I am worn with cares and age,
And just abandoning th' ungrateful stage;
Unprofitably kept at heaven's expense,
I live a rent-charge on his providence:
But you, whom every Muse and Grace adorn,          70
Whom I foresee to better fortune born,
Be kind to my remains; and O defend,
Against your judgement, your departed friend!
Let not th' insulting foe my fame pursue,
But shade those laurels which descend to you:
And take for tribute what these lines express;
You merit more, nor could my love do less.


# Ode on the Death of Mr Henry Purcell,
# Late Servant to His Majesty,
# and Organist of the Chapel Royal,
# and of St Peter's, Westminster


1
Mark how the lark and linnet sing;
    With rival notes
    They strain their warbling throats
    To welcome in the spring.
    But in the close of night,
When Philomel begins her heavenly lay,
    They cease their mutual spite,
Drink in her music with delight,

And listening and silent, and silent and listening, and listening
   and silent obey.

2

So ceased the rival crew when Purcell came;                    10
They sung no more, or only sung his fame.
Struck dumb, they all admired the godlike man:
          The godlike man,
          Alas, too soon retired,
          As he too late began.
We beg beg not hell our Opheus to restore;
          Had he been there,
          Their sovereigns' fear
Had sent him back before.
The power of harmony too well they know:                       20
He long ere this had tuned their jarring sphere,
          And left no hell below.

3

The heavenly choir who heard his notes from high,
Let down the scale of music from the sky;
          They handed him along,
And all the way he taught, and all the way they sung.
   Ye brethren of the lyre and tuneful voice,
   Lament his lot, but at your own rejoice:
Now live secure and linger out your days;
The gods are pleased alone with Purcell's lays,                30
          Nor know to mend their choice.

# from **The Works of Virgil**

## from **The Second Book of the Georgics**

### (1)

*The renewal of the world in spring*

The spring adorns the woods, renews the leaves;
The womb of earth the genial seed receives:
For then almighty Jove descends, and pours                    440
Into his buxom bride his fruitful showers;
And mixing his large limbs with hers, he feeds
Her births with kindly juice and fosters teeming seeds.
Then joyous birds frequent the lonely grove,
And beasts, by Nature stung, renew their love.
Then fields the blades of buried corn disclose;
And while the balmy western spirit blows,
Earth to the breath her bosom dares expose.
With kindly moisture then the plants abound,
The grass securely springs above the ground;                  450
The tender twig shoots upward to the skies,
And on the faith of the new sun relies.
The swerving vines on the tall elms prevail;
Unhurt by southern showers or northern hail,
They spread their gems the genial warmth to share,
And boldly trust their buds in open air.
        In this soft season – let me dare to sing –
The world was hatched by heaven's imperial king:
In prime of all the year, and holidays of spring.
Then did the new creation first appear,                       460
Nor other was the tenour of the year:
When laughing heaven did the great birth attend,
And eastern winds their wintry breath suspend.
Then sheep first saw the sun in open fields,
And savage beasts were sent to stock the wilds;

And golden stars flew up to light the skies,
And man's relentless race from stony quarries rise.
Nor could the tender new creation bear
Th' excessive heats or coldness of the year,
But chilled by winter, or by summer fired,                    470
The middle temper of the spring required,
When warmth and moisture did at once abound,
And heaven's indulgence brooded on the ground.

## (2)

*The consolations of philosophy and the contentments of rural life*

    Happy the man, who, studying nature's laws,
Through known effects can trace the secret cause;
His mind possessing in a quiet state,                         700
Fearless of fortune, and resigned to fate!
And happy too is he who decks the bowers
Of sylvans, and adores the rural powers:
Whose mind, unmoved, the bribes of courts can see,
Their glittering baits and purple slavery;
Nor hopes the people's praise nor fears their frown,
Nor, when contending kindred tear the crown,
Will set up one or pull another down.
    Without concern he hears, but hears from far,
Of tumults and descents and distant war;                      710
Nor with a superstitious fear is awed
For what befalls at home, or what abroad.
Nor envies he the rich their heapy store,
Nor his own peace disturbs with pity for the poor.
He feeds on fruits which, of their own accord,
The willing ground and laden trees afford.
From his loved home no lucre him can draw;
The Senate's mad decrees he never saw;
Nor heard at bawling bars corrupted law.
Some to the seas and some to camps resort,                    720
And some with impudence invade the court:
In foreign countries others seek renown;
With wars and taxes others waste their own,

And houses burn, and household gods deface,
To drink in bowls which glittering gems enchase,
To loll on couches, rich with citron steads,
And lay their guilty limbs in Tyrian beds.
This wretch in earth entombs his golden ore,
Hovering and brooding on his buried store.
Some patriot fools to pop'lar praise aspire,                    730
Or public speeches which worse fools admire,
While from both benches, with redoubled sounds,
Th' applause of lords and commoners abounds.
Some through ambition or through thirst of gold,
Have slain their brothers or their country sold,
And leaving their sweet homes in exile, run
To lands that lie beneath another sun.
    The peasant, innocent of all these ills,
With crooked ploughs the fertile fallows tills,
And the round year with daily labour fills.                     740
From hence the country markets are supplied:
Enough remains for household charge beside,
His wife and tender children to sustain,
And gratefully to feed his dumb, deserving train.
Nor cease his labours till the yellow field
A full return of bearded harvest yield:
A crop so plenteous as the land to load,
O'ercome the crowded barns and lodge on ricks abroad.
Thus every several season is employed,
Some spent in toil, and some in ease enjoyed.                   750
The yeaning ewes prevent the springing year:
The laded boughs their fruits in autumn bear.
'Tis then the vine her liquid harvest yields,
Baked in the sunshine of ascending fields.
The winter comes, and then the falling mast
For greedy swine provides a full repast.
Then olives, ground in mills, their fatness boast,
And winter fruits are mellowed by the frost.
His cares are eased with intervals of bliss;
His little children, climbing for a kiss,                       760
Welcome their father's late return at night;
His faithful bed is crowned with chaste delight.
His kine with swelling udders ready stand,

And, lowing for the pail, invite the milker's hand.
His wanton kids, with budding horns prepared,
Fight harmless battles in his homely yard:
Himself in rustic pomp, on holidays,
To rural powers a just oblation pays,
And on the green his careless limbs displays.
The hearth is in the midst; the herdsmen round                    770
The cheerful fire provoke his health, in goblets crowned.
He calls on Bacchus, and propounds the prize;
The groom his fellow groom at butts defies,
And bends his bow, and levels with his eyes;
Or stripped for wrestling smears his limbs with oil,
And watches with a trip his foe to foil.

# from **The Third Book of the Georgics**

*The universal power of sexual passion*

Thus every creature, and of every kind,
The secret joys of sweet coition find:
Not only man's imperial race, but they
That wing the liquid air or swim the sea,
Or haunt the desert, rush into the flame:
For Love is lord of all and is in all the same.                   380
    'Tis with this rage the mother lion stung,
Scours o'er the plain regardless of her young:
Demanding rites of love she sternly stalks,
And hunts her lover in his lonely walks.
'Tis then the shapeless bear his den forsakes;
In woods and fields a wild destruction makes.
Boars whet their tusks, to battle tigers move,
Enraged with hunger, more enraged with love.
    Then woe to him that in the desert land
Of Libya travels o'er the burning sand!                           390
The stallion snuffs the well-known scent afar,
And snorts and trembles for the distant mare;

Nor bits nor bridles can his rage restrain,
And rugged rocks are interposed in vain:
He makes his way o'er mountains, and contemns
Unruly torrents and unforded streams.
The bristled boar who feels the pleasing wound
New grinds his arming tusks and digs the ground.
The sleepy lecher shuts his little eyes;
About his churning chaps the frothy bubbles rise:                  400
He rubs his sides against a tree, prepares
And hardens both his shoulders for the wars.

What did the youth, when love's unerring dart
Transfixed his liver and inflamed his heart?
Alone, by night, his watery way he took;
About him and above the billows broke;
The sluices of the skies were open spread,
And rolling thunder rattled o'er his head;
The raging tempest called him back in vain,
And every boding omen of the main:                                 410
Nor could his kindred, nor the kindly force
Of weeping parents change his fatal course;
No, not the dying maid, who must deplore
His floating carcass on the Sestian shore.

I pass the wars that spotted lynxes make
With their fierce rivals for the females' sake,
The howling wolves', the mastiffs' amorous rage;
When ev'n the fearful stag dares for his hind engage.
But far above the rest, the furious mare,
Barred from the male, is frantic with despair:                     420
For when her pouting vent declares her pain,
She tears the harness and she rends the rein.
For this (when Venus gave them rage and power)
Their master's mangled members they devour,
Of love defrauded in their longing hour.
For love they force through thickets of the wood,
They climb the steepy hills and stem the flood.

# from **The Fourth Book of the Georgics**

*Civil war in the beehive*

But if intestine broils alarm the hive
(For two pretenders oft for empire strive),
The vulgar in divided factions jar;
And murmuring sounds proclaim the civil war.
Inflamed with ire, and trembling with disdain,
Scarce can their limbs their mighty souls contain.
With shouts the cowards' courage they excite,
And martial clangours call them out to fight;
With hoarse alarms the hollow camp rebounds,     100
That imitates the trumpet's angry sounds;
Then to their common standard they repair;
The nimble horsemen scour the fields of air;
In form of battle drawn, they issue forth,
And every knight is proud to prove his worth.
Pressed for their country's honour, and their king's,
On their sharp beaks they whet their pointed stings,
And exercise their arms, and tremble with their wings.
Full in the midst the haughty monarchs ride;
The trusty guards come up and close the side;     110
With shouts the daring foe to battle is defied.
Thus in the season of unclouded spring
To war they follow their undaunted king,
Crowd through their gates, and in the fields of light
The shocking squadrons meet in mortal fight.
Headlong they fall from high, and wounded wound,
And heaps of slaughtered soldiers bite the ground.
Hard hailstones lie not thicker on the plain,
Nor shaken oaks such showers of acorns rain.
    With gorgeous wings, the marks of sov'reign sway,     120
The two contending princes make their way;
Intrepid through the midst of danger go,
Their friends encourage, and amaze the foe.
With mighty souls in narrow bodies pressed
They challenge, and encounter breast to breast;
So fixed on fame, unknowing how to fly,

And obstinately bent to win or die,
That long the doubtful combat they maintain,
Till one prevails – for one can only reign.
Yet all those dreadful deeds, this deadly fray,          130
A cast of scattered dust will soon allay,
And undecided leave the fortune of the day.
When both the chiefs are sundered from the fight,
Then to the lawful king restore his right;
And let the wasteful prodigal be slain,
That he who best deserves alone may reign.

# from **The Second Book of the Aeneis**

*Having escaped the sack of Troy, Aeneas embarks on his divinely
ordained mission to found a Trojan settlement in Italy. After a storm at
sea, he is hospitably received by Dido, Queen of Carthage, to whom he
narrates the fall of Troy and the death of Priam.*

'Perhaps you may of Priam's fate enquire.
He, when he saw his regal town on fire,
His ruined palace and his entering foes,
On every side inevitable woes,
In arms disused invests his limbs, decayed
Like them with age, a late and useless aid.
His feeble shoulders scarce the weight sustain:
Loaded, not armed, he creeps along with pain,
Despairing of success, ambitious to be slain.
    Uncovered but by heaven, there stood in view          700
An altar: near the hearth a laurel grew,
Doddered with age, whose boughs encompass round
The household gods, and shade the holy ground.
Here Hecuba with all her helpless train
Of dames for shelter sought, but sought in vain.
Driv'n like a flock of doves along the sky,
Their images they hug, and to their altars fly.
The Queen, when she beheld her trembling lord,

And hanging by his side a heavy sword,
"What rage," she cried, "has seized my husband's mind?        710
What arms are these, and to what use designed?
These times want other aids: were Hector here,
Ev'n Hector now in vain, like Priam, would appear.
With us one common shelter thou shalt find,
Or in one common fate with us be joined."
She said, and with a last salute embraced
The poor old man, and by the laurel placed.
    Behold Polites, one of Priam's sons,
Pursued by Pyrrhus there for safety runs.
Through swords and foes amazed and hurt, he flies        720
Through empty courts and open galleries.
Him Pyrrhus, urging with his lance, pursues,
And often reaches, and his thrusts renews.
The youth transfixed, with lamentable cries
Expires before his wretched parent's eyes:
Whom gasping at his feet when Priam saw,
The fear of death gave place to nature's law,
And shaking more with anger than with age,
"The gods," said he, "requite thy brutal rage –
As sure they will, barbarian, sure they must,        730
If there be gods in heaven, and gods be just –
Who tak'st in wrongs an insolent delight;
With a son's death t' infest a father's sight.
Not he, whom thou and lying Fame conspire
To call thee his; not he, thy vaunted sire,
Thus used my wretched age: the gods he feared;
The laws of nature and of nations heard.
He cheered my sorrows, and for sums of gold
The bloodless carcass of my Hector sold;
Pitied the woes a parent underwent,        740
And sent me back in safety from his tent."
    This said, his feeble hand a javelin threw,
Which, fluttering, seemed to loiter as it flew:
Just, and but barely, to the mark it held,
And faintly tinkled on the brazen shield.
    Then Pyrrhus thus: "Go thou from me to Fate,
And to my father my foul deeds relate:
Now die!" With that, he dragged the trembling sire,

Sliddering through clottered blood and holy mire
(The mingled paste his murdered son had made),                    750
Hauled from beneath the violated shade,
And on the sacred pile the royal victim laid.
His right hand held his bloody falchion bare,
His left he twisted in his hoary hair;
Then with a speeding thrust his heart he found;
The lukewarm blood came rushing through the wound,
And sanguine streams distained the sacred ground.
   Thus Priam fell, and shared one common fate
With Troy in ashes, and his ruined state:
He who the sceptre of all Asia swayed,                           760
Whom monarchs like domestic slaves obeyed.
On the bleak shore now lies th' abandoned king,
A headless carcass and a nameless thing.'

# from **The Fourth Book of the Aeneis**

## (1)

*Dido is consumed with an unequenchable passion for Aeneas.*

Sick with desire, and seeking him she loves,
From street to street the raving Dido roves.
So when the watchful shepherd, from the blind,
Wounds with a random shaft the careless hind,
Distracted with her pain she flies the woods,
Bounds o'er the lawn and seeks the silent floods,
With fruitless care; for still the fatal dart
Sticks in her side and rankles in her heart.                     100
And now she leads the Trojan chief along
The lofty walls, amidst the busty throng;
Displays her Tyrian wealth and rising town,
Which love, without his labour, makes his own.
This pomp she shows to tempt her wandering guest;
Her faltering tongue forbids to speak the rest.

When day declines, and feasts renew the night,
Still on his face she feeds her famished sight;
She longs again to hear the Prince relate
His own adventures and the Trojan fate.          110
He tells it o'er and o'er, but still in vain,
For still she begs to hear it once again.
The hearer on the speaker's mouth depends,
And thus the tragic story never ends.

## (2)

*Fame spreads the news of Dido's consummated love.*

The louds reports through Lybian cities goes;
Fame, the great ill, from small beginnings grows;
Swift from the first, and every moment brings
New vigour to her flights, new pinions to her wings.
Soon grows the pigmy to gigantic size,
Her feet on earth, her forehead in the skies:
Enraged against the gods, revengeful Earth
Produced her last of the Titanian birth.
Swift is her walk, more swift her wingèd haste,
A monstrous phantom, horrible and vast;          260
As many plumes as raise her lofty flight,
So many piercing eyes enlarge her sight:
Millions of opening mouths to Fame belong;
And every mouth is furnished with a tongue;
And round with listening ears the flying plague is hung.
She fills the peaceful universe with cries;
No slumbers ever close her wakeful eyes.
By day from lofty towers her head she shows,
And spreads through trembling crowds disastrous news.
With court informers haunts, and royal spies,          270
Things done relates, not done she feigns, and mingles truth
     with lies.
Talk is her business, and her chief delight
To tell of prodigies, and cause affright.
   She fills the people's ears with Dido's name,
Who, lost to honour and the sense of shame,
Admits into her throne and nuptial bed

A wandering guest who from his country fled:
Whole days with him she passes in delights,
And wastes in luxury long winter nights;
Forgetful of her fame and royal trust,                          280
Dissolved in ease, abandoned to her lust.

### (3)

*Commanded by Mercury to pursue his mission, Aeneas resolves to
leave Carthage. When Dido hears, she upbraids him for his treachery
and ingratitude, and prophesies that her shade will haunt him.*

'False as thou art, and more than false, foresworn,
Not sprung from noble blood, nor goddess-born,
But hewn from hardened entrails of a rock,
And rough Hyrcanian tigers gave thee suck.
Why should I fawn, what worse have I to fear?
Did he once look, or lent a listening ear;
Sighed when I sobbed, or shed one kindly tear?
All symptoms of a base, ungrateful mind,
So foul that which is worse 'tis hard to find.                   530
   Of man's injustice, why should I complain?
The gods, and Jove himself behold in vain
Triumphant treason, yet no thunder flies,
Nor Juno views my wrongs with equal eyes:
Faithless is earth, and faithless are the skies!
Justice is fled, and Truth is now no more.
   I saved the shipwrecked exile on my shore,
With needful food his hungry Trojans fed;
I took the traitor to my throne and bed,
Fool that I was – 'tis little to repeat                          540
The rest – I stored and rigged his ruined fleet.
I rave! I rave! A god's command he pleads,
And makes heav'n áccessory to his deeds.
Now Lycian lots, and now the Delian god,
Now Hermes is employed from Jove's abode,
To warn him hence – as if the peaceful state
Of heavenly powers were touched with human fate!
   But go! Thy flight no longer I detain.

Go, seek thy promised kingdom through the main:
Yet if the heavens will hear my pious vow,                    550
The faithless waves, not half as false as thou,
Or secret sands shall sepulchres afford
To thy proud vessels and their perjured lord.
Then shalt thou call on injured Dido's name;
Dido shall come, in a black sulph'ry flame,
When death has one dissolved her mortal frame;
Shall smile to see the traitor vainly weep;
Her angry ghost arising from the deep
Shall haunt thee waking, and disturb thy sleep.
At least my shade thy punishment shall know,                 560
And Fame shall spread the pleasing news below.'

## (4)

*Despite Dido's renewed pleas, Aeneas remains steadfast in his resolve*
*to leave Carthage.*

As when the winds their airy quarrel try,
Jostling from every quarter of the sky,
This way and that the mountain oak they bend,               640
His boughs they shatter, and his branches rend;
With leaves and falling mast they spread the ground;
The hollow valleys echo to the sound.
Unmoved, the royal plant their fury mocks,
Or shaken, clings more closely to the rocks:
Far as he shoots his towering head on high,
So deep in earth his fixed foundations lie.
No less a storm the Trojan hero bears;
Thick messages and loud complaints he hears,
And bandied words still beating on his ears.                 650
Sighs, groans, and tears proclaim his inward pains;
But the firm purpose of his heart remains.

# from **The Eighth Book of the Aeneis**

*When the Trojans reach Italy, Juno stirs up hostility against them.*
*The Italian tribes, led by Turnus, King of the Rutulians, take up arms*
*against the Trojans. Venus persuades her husband, the smith-god*
*Vulcan, to forge arms for Aeneas.*

Now Night had shed her silver dews around,
And with her sable wings embraced the ground,
When love's fair goddess, anxious for her son
(New tumults rising and new wars begun),
Couched with her husband in his golden bed,
With these alluring words invokes his aid;
And, that her pleasing speech his mind may move,       490
Inspires each accent with the charms of love:
    'While cruel Fate conspired with Grecian powers
To level with the ground the Trojan towers,
I asked not aid th' unhappy to restore,
Nor did the succour of thy skill implore;
Nor urged the labours of my lord in vain,
A sinking empire longer to sustain;
Though much I owed to Priam's house, and more
The dangers of Aeneas did deplore.
But now by Jove's command and Fate's decree          500
His race is doomed to reign in Italy;
With humble suit I beg thy needful art,
O still-propitious power that rules my heart!
A mother kneels a suppliant for her son.
By Thetis and Aurora thou wert won
To forge impenetrable shields, and grace
With fated arms a less illustrious race.
Behold, what haughty nations are combined
Against the relics of the Phrygian kind,
With fire and sword my people to destroy,            510
And conquer Venus twice, in conquering Troy.'
    She said, and straight her arms of snowy hue
About her unresolving husband threw.
Her soft embraces soon infuse desire,

His bones and marrow sudden warmth inspire,
And all the godhead feels the wonted fire.
Not half so swift the rattling thunder flies,
Or forky lightnings flash along the skies.
The goddess, proud of her successful wiles
And conscious of her form, in secret smiles.          520
Then thus the power, obnoxious to her charms,
Panting and half dissolving in her arms:
    'Why seek you reasons for a cause so just,
Or your own beauties or my love distrust?
Long since had you required my helpful hand,
Th' artificer and art you might command
To labour arms for Troy: nor Jove, nor Fate
Confined their empire to so short a date.
And if you now desire new wars to wage,
My skill I promise and my pains engage.          530
Whatever melting metals can conspire,
Or breathing bellows, or the forming fire,
Is freely yours: your anxious fears remove,
And think no task is difficult to love.'
    Trembling he spoke, and, eager of her charms,
He snatched the willing goddess to his arms;
Till in her lap infused he lay possessed
Of full desire, and sunk to pleasing rest.
    Now when the Night her middle race had rode,
And his first slumber had refreshed the god;          540
The time when early housewives leave the bed;
When living embers on the hearth they spread,
Supply the lamp and call the maids to rise;
With yawning mouths and with half-opened eyes
They ply the distaff by the winking light,
And to their daily labour add the night:
Thus frugally they earn their children's bread,
And uncorrupted keep the nuptial bed;
Not less concerned, nor at a later hour,
Rose from his downy couch the forging power.          550

# from **The Ninth Book of the Aeneis**

*The Trojan warrior Nisus and his young friend Euryalus set out for*
*the Latin camp. Having surprised the Latins in a drunken sleep, they*
*kill many of their number. As they return, they are sighted by*
*Volscens, who is bringing reinforcements for Turnus.*

But far they had not passed, before they spied
Three hundred horse, with Volscens for their guide.
The Queen a legion to King Turnus sent,
But the swift horse the slower foot outwent,
And now, advancing, sought the leader's tent.
They saw the pair, for through the doubtful shade
His shining helm Euryalus betrayed,
On which the moon with full reflection played.
   "Tis not for nought,' cried Volscens from the crowd,
'These men go there,' then raised his voice aloud:          510
'Stand, stand! Why thus in arms? And whither bent?
From whence, to whom, and on what errand sent?'
Silent they scud away, and haste their flight
To neighbouring woods, and trust themselves to night.
The speedy horse all passages belay,
And spur their smoking steeds to cross their way,
And watch each entrance of the winding wood.
Black was the forest, thick with beech it stood,
Horrid with fern, and intricate with thorn;
Few paths of human feet or tracks of beasts were worn.          520
The darkness of the shades, his heavy prey,
And fear, misled the younger from his way;
But Nisus hit the turns with happier haste,
And thoughtless of his friend the forest passed,
And Alban plains (from Alba's name so called)
Where King Latinus then his oxen stalled;
Till turning at the length, he stood his ground,
And missed his friend, and cast his eyes around.
   'Ah wretch!' he cried, 'where have I left behind
Th' unhappy youth? Where shall I hope to find?          530
Or what way to take?' Again he ventures back,
And treads the mazes of his former track.
He winds the wood, and, listening, hears the noise

Of trampling coursers, and the riders' voice.
The sound approached, and suddenly he viewed
The foes enclosing, and his friend pursued,
Forelaid, and taken, while he strove in vain
The shelter of the friendly shades to gain.
What should he next attempt, what arms employ,
What fruitless force, to free the captive boy?                           540
Or desperate should he rush and lose his life,
With odds oppressed, in such unequal strife?
      Resolved at length, his pointed spear he shook,
And casting on the moon a mournful look,
'Guardian of groves, and goddess of the night,
Fair Queen!' he said, 'direct my dart aright.
If e'er my pious father for my sake
Did grateful offerings on thy altars make,
Or I increased them with my sylvan toils,
And hung thy holy roofs with savage spoils,                              550
Give me to scatter these!' Then from his ear
He poised, and aimed, and launched the trembling spear.
The deadly weapon, hissing from the grove,
Impetuous on the back of Sulmo drove;
Pierced his thin armour, drank his vital blood,
And in his body left the broken wood.
He staggers round, his eyeballs roll in death,
And with short sobs he gasps away his breath.
All stand amazed; a second javelin flies
With equal strength, and quivers through the skies.                      560
This through thy temples, Tagus, forced the way,
And in the brain-pan warmly buried lay.
Fierce Volscens foams with rage, and gazing round
Descried not him who gave the fatal wound,
Nor knew to fix revenge. 'But thou,' he cries,
'Shalt pay for both,' and at the prisoner flies
With his drawn sword. Then, struck with deep despair,
That cruel sight the lover could not bear,
But from his covert rushed in open view,
And sent his voice before him as he flew:                                570
      'Me, me!' he cried, 'turn all your swords alone
On me: the fact confessed, the fault my own.
He neither could nor durst, the guiltless youth:

Ye moon and stars bear witness to the truth!
His only crime – if friendship can offend –
Is too much love to his unhappy friend.'
   Too late he speaks; the sword, which fury guides,
Driv'n with full force had pierced his tender sides.
Down fell the beauteous youth; the yawning wound
Gushed out a purple stream and stained the ground.          580
His snowy neck reclines upon his breast,
Like a fair flower by the keen share oppressed,
Like a white poppy sinking on the plain,
Whose heavy head is overcharged with rain.
Despair, and rage, and vengeance justly vowed,
Drove Nisus headlong on the hostile crowd;
Volscens he seeks, on him alone he bends,
Borne back and bored by his surrounding friends,
Onward he pressed and kept him still in sight,
Then whirled aloft his sword with all his might:          590
Th' unerring steel descended while he spoke,
Pierced his wide mouth and through his weazon broke.
Dying, he slew; and staggering on the plain,
With swimming eyes he sought his lover slain;
Then quiet on his bleeding bosom fell,
Content in death to be revenged so well.
   O happy friends – for if my verse can give
Immortal life, your fame shall ever live!
Fixed as the Capitol's foundation lies,
And spread where'er the Roman eagle flies.          600

# Alexander's Feast, or The Power of Music:
# An Ode in Honour of St Cecilia's Day

### 1

'Twas at the royal feast for Persia won
　　　By Philip's warlike son;
　　　Aloft in awful state
　　　The godlike hero sate
　　　　　On his imperial throne;
His valiant peers were placed around,
Their brows with roses and with myrtles bound
　　(So should desert in arms be crowned);
The lovely Thais by his side
Sate like a blooming eastern bride,　　　　　　　　　　10
In flower of youth and beauty's pride:
　　　Happy, happy, happy pair!
　　　None but the brave,
　　　None but the brave,
　　　None but the brave deserves the fair!

### CHORUS

*Happy, happy, happy pair!*
*None but the brave,*
*None but the brave,*
*None but the brave deserves the fair!*

### 2

Timotheus placed on high　　　　　　　　　　　　　　20
　　Amid the tuneful choir
　　With flying fingers touched the lyre:
The trembling notes ascend the sky
　　　　　And heavenly joys inspire.
The song began from Jove
Who left his blissful seats above,
Such is the power of mighty love!
A dragon's fiery form belied the god;
Sublime on radiant spires he rode,
　　　When he to fair Olympia pressed,　　　　　　　　30

And while he sought her snowy breast:
Then round her slender waist he curled,
And stamped an image of himself, a sovereign of the world.
The listening crowd admire the lofty sound;
A present deity! they shout around:
A present deity! the vaulted roofs rebound:
                    With ravished ears
                    The monarch hears,
                    Assumes the god,
                    Affects to nod,                              40
And seems to shake the spheres.


*CHORUS*
*With ravished ears*
*The monarch hears,*
*Assumes the god,*
*Affects to nod,*
*And seems to shake the spheres.*


3
The praise of Bacchus then the sweet musician sung,
        Of Bacchus ever fair and ever young:
            The jolly god in triumph comes;
            Sound the trumpets, beat the drums!          50
            Flushed with a purple grace
            He shows his honest face:
Now give the hautboys breath: he comes, he comes!
        Bacchus, ever fair and young,
            Drinking joys did first ordain;
        Bacchus' blessings are a treasure,
        Drinking is the soldier's pleasure:
                Rich the treasure,
                Sweet the pleasure,
                Sweet is pleasure after pain.              60


*CHORUS*
*Bacchus' blessings are a treasure,*
*Drinking is the soldier's pleasure:*
        *Rich the treasure,*

*Sweet the pleasure,*
*Sweet is pleasure after pain.*

### 4

Soothed with the sound the king grew vain;
　　Fought all his battles o'er again,
And thrice he routed all his foes, and thrice he slew the slain.
　　　　The master saw the madness rise,
　　　　His glowing cheeks, his ardent eyes,          70
　　　　And while he heaven and earth defied,
　　　　Changed his hand and checked his pride.
　　　　　He chose a mournful Muse
　　　　　Soft pity to infuse:
　　　　He sung Darius great and good,
　　　　　By too severe a fate
　　　　Fallen, fallen, fallen, fallen,
　　　　　Fallen from his high estate,
　　　　　And weltering in his blood;
Deserted at his utmost need          80
By those his former bounty fed;
On the bare earth exposed he lies,
With not a friend to close his eyes.

　　　With downcast looks the joyless victor sate,
　　　　Revolving in his altered soul
　　　　　The various turns of chance below;
　　　　And now and then a sigh he stole,
　　　　　And tears began to flow.

### CHORUS

*Revolving in his altered soul*
　*The various turns of chance below;*          90
*And now and then a sigh he stole,*
　*And tears began to flow.*

### 5

The mighty master smiled to see
That love was in the next degree;
'Twas but a kindred-sound to move,
For pity melts the mind to love.

Softly sweet, in Lydian measures,
Soon he soothed his soul to pleasures.
War, he sung, is toil and trouble,
Honour but an empty bubble;                          100
    Never ending, still beginning,
Fighting still, and still destroying;
    If the world be worth thy winning,
Think, O think, it worth enjoying:
    Lovely Thais sits beside thee,
    Take the good the gods provide thee.

The many rend the skies with loud applause;
So Love was crowned, but Music won the cause.
    The prince, unable to conceal his pain,
        Gazed on the fair                    110
        Who caused his care,
    And sighed and looked, sighed and looked,
Sighed and looked, and sighed again:
At length, with love and wine at once oppressed,
The vanquished victor sunk upon her breast.

### CHORUS

*The prince, unable to conceal his pain,*
    *Gazed on the fair*
    *Who caused his care,*
    *And sighed and looked, sighed and looked,*
*Sighed and looked, and sighed again:*                120
*At length, with love and wine at once oppressed.*
*The vanquished victor sunk upon her breast.*

6

Now strike the golden lyre again:
A louder yet, and yet a louder strain!
Break his bands of sleep asunder
And rouse him like a rattling peal of thunder.
    Hark, hark! the horrid sound
      Has raised up his head:
      As awaked from the dead
    And amazed he stares around.                 130
Revenge, revenge, Timotheus cries,
See the Furies arise!

See the snakes that they rear,
How they hiss in their hair,
And the sparkles that flash from their eyes!
Behold a ghastly band,
Each a torch in his hand!
Those are Grecian ghosts, that in battle were slain
And unburied remain
Inglorious on the plain:     140
Give the vengeance due
To the valiant crew!
Behold how they toss their torches on high,
How they point to the Persian abodes
And glittering temples of their hostile gods.
The princes applaud with a furious joy:
And the King seized a flambeau with zeal to destroy;
Thais led the way
To light him to his prey,
And like another Helen, fired another Troy.     150

*CHORUS*

*And the King seized a flambeau with zeal to destroy;*
*Thais led the way*
*To light him to his prey,*
*And like another Helen, fired another Troy.*

7

Thus, long ago,
Ere heaving bellows learned to blow,
While organs yet were mute,
Timotheus, to his breathing flute
And sounding lyre,
Could swell the soul to rage, or kindle soft desire.     160
At last divine Cecilia came,
Inventress of the vocal frame;
The sweet enthusiast from her sacred store
Enlarged the former narrow bounds,
And added length to solemn sounds,
With nature's mother wit and arts unknown before.
Let old Timotheus yield the prize,
Or both divide the crown;

He raised a mortal to the skies;
She drew an angel down.                                    170


GRAND CHORUS
At last divine Cecilia came,
Inventress of the vocal frame;
The sweet enthusiast from her sacred store
Enlarged the former narrow bounds,
And added length to solemn sounds,
With nature's mother wit, and arts unknown before.
Let old Timotheus yield the prize
Or both divide the crown;
He raised a mortal to the skies;
She drew an angel down.                                    180

# from **Fables Ancient and Modern**

## from **Palamon and Arcite,**
## **or The Knight's Tale, from Chaucer**

*Palamon and Arcite, two young knights, are held prisoner by Theseus in
a tower from which they see Emily, and both fall in love with her. Arcite
has been killed in a tournament, fighting for Emily's hand. A year later,
Theseus summons Palamon and Emily and proposes that they marry,
offering them consolation for sufferings past.*

'The cause and spring of motion from above
Hung down on earth the golden chain of love;
Great was th' effect and high was his intent,
When peace among the jarring seeds he sent.
Fire, flood, and earth, and air by this were bound,
And love, the common link, the new creation crowned.
The chain still holds; for though the forms decay,      1030
Eternal matter never wears away:
The same First Mover certain bounds has placed
How long those perishable forms shall last;
Nor can they last beyond the time assigned
By that all-seeing and all-making mind:
Shorten their hours they may, for will is free,
But never pass th' appointed destiny.
So men oppressed, when weary of their breath,
Throw off the burden and suborn their death.
Then since those forms begin and have their end,      1040
On some unaltered cause they sure depend:
Parts of the whole are we, but God the whole,
Who gives us life and animating soul.
For nature cannot from a part derive
That being which the whole can only give:
He perfect, stable, but imperfect we,
Subject to change, and different in degree:
Plants, beasts and man; and as our organs are,

We more or less of his perfection share.
But by a long descent th' ethereal fire                              1050
Corrupts; and forms, the mortal part, expire:
As he withdraws his virtue, so they pass,
And the same matter makes another mass.
    This law th' Omniscient Power was pleased to give,
That every kind should by succession live;
That individuals die, his will ordains;
The propagated species still remains.
The monarch oak, the patriarch of the trees,
Shoots rising up, and spreads by slow degrees;
Three centuries he grows, and three he stays,                         1060
Supreme in state, and in three more decays:
So wears the paving pebble in the street,
And towns and towers their fatal periods meet.
So rivers, rapid once, now naked lie,
Forsaken of their springs, and leave their channels dry;
So man, at first a drop, dilates with heat,
Then formed, the little heart begins to beat;
Secret he feeds, unknowing in the cell;
At length, for hatching ripe, he breaks the shell,
And struggles into breath, and cries for aid;                        1070
Then helpless in his mother's lap is laid.
He creeps, he walks, and issuing into man,
Grudges their life from whence his own began;
Retchless of laws, affects to rule alone,
Anxious to reign, and restless on the throne;
First vegetive, then feels, and reasons last;
Rich of three souls, and lives all three to waste.
Some thus, but thousands more in flower of age;
For few arrive to run the latter stage.
Sunk in the first, in battle some are slain,                         1080
And others whelmed beneath the stormy main.
What makes all this but Jupiter the King,
At whose command we perish and we spring?
    Then 'tis our best, since thus ordained to die,
To make a virtue of necessity;
Take what he gives, since to rebel is vain;
The bad grows better which we well sustain;

And could we choose the time and choose aright,
'Tis best to die, our honour at the height,
When we have done our ancestors no shame,                    1090
But served our friends and well secured our fame;
Then should we wish our happy life to close,
And leave no more for Fortune to dispose.
So should we make our death a glad relief
From future shame, from sickness, and from grief;
Enjoying while we live the present hour,
And dying in our excellence and flower.
Then round our death-bed every friend should run,
And joy us of our conquest early won:
While the malicious world, with envious tears,               1100
Should grudge our happy end and wish it theirs.
    Since then our Arcite is with honour dead,
Why should we mourn that he so soon is freed,
Or call untimely what the gods decreed?
With grief as just a friend may be deplored,
From a foul prison to free air restored.
Ought he to thank his kinsman or his wife,
Could tears recall him into wretched life?
Their sorrow hurts themselves, on him is lost;
And worse than both, offends his happy ghost.               1110
What then remains, but after past annoy
To take the good vicissitude of joy;
To thank the gracious gods for what they give,
Possess our souls, and while we live, to live?'

# from **Sigismonda and Guiscardo,**
# **from Boccace**

*Sigismonda, a young widow, has contracted a secret marriage with*
*Guiscardo, squire to her father, Tancred. Tancred has had Guiscardo*
*arrested, and has rebuked Sigismonda for her conduct. She responds to*
*his charges.*

'Tancred, I neither am disposed to make                                390
Request for life, nor offered life to take:
Much less deny the deed; but least of all
Beneath pretended justice weakly fall.
My words to sacred truth shall be confined;
My deeds shall show the greatness of my mind.
That I have loved, I own; that still I love,
I call to witness all the powers above.
Yet more I own: to Guiscard's love I give
The small remaining time I have to live;
And if beyond this life desire can be,                                  400
Not Fate itself shall set my passion free.
    This first avowed, nor folly warped my mind,
Nor the frail texture of the female kind
Betrayed my virtue; for too well I knew
What honour was, and honour had his due:
Before the holy priest my vows were tied,
So came I not a strumpet, but a bride.
This for my fame, and for the public voice:
Yet more, his merits justified my choice:
Which had they not, the first election thine,                          410
That bond dissolved, the next is freely mine:
Or grant I erred – which yet I must deny –
Had parents power ev'n second vows to tie,
Thy little care to mend my widowed nights
Has forced me to recourse of marriage rites,
To fill an empty side, and follow known delights.
What have I done in this deserving blame?
State laws may alter: nature's are the same;
Those are usurped on helpless womankind,
Made without our consent, and wanting power to bind.                    420

Thou, Tancred, better shouldst have understood,
That, as thy father gave thee flesh and blood,
So gav'st thou me: not from the quarry hewed,
But of a softer mould, with sense endued;
Ev'n softer than thy own, of suppler kind,
More exquisite of taste, and more than man refined.
Nor need'st thou by thy daughter to be told,
Though now thy sprightly blood with age be cold;
Thou hast been young, and canst remember still,
That when thou hadst the power thou hadst the will;    430
And from the past experience of thy fires,
Canst tell with what a tide our strong desires
Come rushing on in youth, and what their rage requires.
   And grant thy youth was exercised in arms,
When love no leisure found for softer charms,
My tender age in luxury was trained,
With idle ease and pageants entertained;
My hours my own, my pleasures unrestrained.
So bred, no wonder if I took the bent
That seemed ev'n warranted by thy consent;    440
For when the father is too fondly kind,
Such seed he sows, such harvest shall he find.
   Blame then thyself, as reason's law requires
(Since nature gave, and thou foment'st my fires),
If still those appetites continue strong.
Thou may'st consider, I am yet but young:
Consider too, that having been a wife,
I must have tasted of a better life,
And am not to be blamed if I renew
By lawful means the joys which then I knew.    450
Where was the crime if pleasure I procured,
Young, and a woman, and to bliss inured?
That was my case, and this is my defence:
I pleased myself, I shunned incontinence,
And, urged by strong desires, indulged my sense.'

# from **Baucis and Philemon, out of the Eighth Book of Ovid's** *Metamorphoses*

*Jupiter and Mercury, who are visiting the earth* incognito, *are welcomed to a rustic meal in the humble dwelling of an aged couple, Baucis and Philemon.*

From lofty roofs the gods repulsed before,
Now stooping entered through the little door;
The man, their hearty welcome first expressed,
A common settle drew for either guest,
Inviting each his weary limbs to rest.
But ere they sat, officious Baucis lays
Two cushions stuffed with straw, the seat to raise –
Coarse, but the best she had – then rakes the load
Of ashes from the hearth, and spreads abroad
The living coals, and, lest they should expire,                       50
With leaves and barks she feeds her infant fire.
It smokes, and then with trembling breath she blows,
Till in a cheerful blaze the flames arose.
With brushwood and with chips she strengthens these,
And adds at last the boughs of rotten trees.
The fire thus formed, she sets the kettle on;
Like burnished gold the little seether shone;
Next took the coleworts which her husband got
From his own ground, a small, well-watered spot;
She stripped the stalks of all their leaves; the best      60
She culled, and then with handy-care she dressed.
   High o'er the hearth a chine of bacon hung;
Good old Philemon seized it with a prong,
And from the sooty rafter drew it down,
Then cut a slice, but scarce enough for one,
Yet a large portion of a little store,
Which for their sakes alone he wished were more.
This in the pot he plunged without delay,
To tame the flesh and drain the salt away.
The time between, before the fire they sat,                    70
And shortened the delay by pleasing chat.
   A beam there was, on which a beechen pail

Hung by the handle on a driven nail;
This filled with water gently warmed they set
Before their guests; in this they bathed their feet,
And after with clean towels dried their sweat:
This done, the host produced the genial bed,
Sallow the feet, the borders and the stead,
Which with no costly coverlet they spread,
But coarse old garments; yet such robes as these          80
They laid alone at feasts, on holidays.
The good old housewife, tucking up her gown,
The table sets; th' invited gods lie down.
The trivet-table of a foot was lame,
A blot which prudent Baucis overcame,
Who thrust beneath the limping leg a sherd,
So was the mended board exactly reared;
Then rubbed it o'er with newly-gathered mint,
A wholesome herb that breathed a grateful scent.
    Pallas began the feast, where first was seen          90
The party-coloured olive, black and green;
Autumnal cornels next in order served,
In lees of wine well pickled and preserved;
A garden-salad was the third supply,
Of endive, radishes and succory:
Then curds and cream, the flower of country fare,.
And new-laid eggs, which Baucis' busy care
Turned by a gentle fire, and roasted rare.
All these in earthenware were served to board;
And next in place an earthen pitcher, stored          100
With liquor of the best the cottage could afford.
This was the table's ornament and pride,
With figures wrought; like pages at his side
Stood beechen bowls, and these were shining clean,
Varnished with wax without, and lined within.
By this the boiling kettle had prepared,
And to the table sent the smoking lard;
On which with eager appetite they dine,
A savoury bit that served to relish wine;
The wine itself was suiting to the rest,          110
Still working in the must and lately pressed.
    The second course succeeds like that before;

Plums, apples, nuts, and of their wintry store,
Dry figs, and grapes and wrinkled dates were set
In canisters t' enlarge the little treat;
All these a milk-white honeycomb surround,
Which in the midst the country banquet crowned.
But the kind hosts their entertainment grace
With hearty welcome and an open face;
In all they did, you might discern with ease                    120
A willing mind, and a desire to please.
   Meantime the beechen bowls went round, and still,
Though often emptied, were observed to fill;
Filled without hands, and of their own accord
Ran without feet, and danced about the board.
Devotion seized the pair, to see the feast
With wine, and of no common grape, increased;
And up they held their hands, and fell to prayer,
Excusing as they could their country fare.
   One goose they had – 'twas all they could allow –              130
A wakeful sentry, and on duty now,
Whom to the gods for sacrifice they vow.
Her with malicious zeal the couple viewed;
She ran for life, and limping they pursued:
Full well the fowl perceived their bad intent,
And would not make her masters' compliment,
But persecuted to the powers she flies,
And close between the legs of Jove she lies.
He with a gracious ear the suppliant heard,
And saved her life; then what he was declared,                  140
And owned the god. 'The neighbourhood,' said he,
'Shall justly perish for impiety.
You stand alone exempted, but obey
With speed, and follow where we lead the way:
Leave these accursed, and to the mountain's height
Ascend, nor once look backward in your flight.'

# from **Cinyras and Myrrha, out of the Tenth Book of Ovid's** *Metamorphoses*

*Myrrha, daughter of Cinyras, King of Cyprus, has been smitten with an incestuous passion for her father. She meditates on her plight.*

'Ah, Myrrha, whither would thy wishes tend?
Ye gods, ye sacred laws, my soul defend
From such a crime as all mankind detest,
And never lodged before in human breast!
But is it sin? Or makes my mind alone
Th' imagined sin? For Nature makes it none.       40
What tyrant then these envious laws began,
Made not for any other beast but man?
The father-bull his daughter may bestride,
The horse may make his mother-mare a bride;
What piety forbids the lusty ram
Or more salacious goat to rut their dam?
The hen is free to wed the chick she bore,
And make a husband whom she hatched before.
All creatures else are of a happier kind,
Whom nor ill-natured laws from pleasures bind,       50
Nor thoughts of sin disturb their peace of mind.
    But man a slave of his own making lives:
The fool denies himself what Nature gives;
Too busy senates, with an over-care
To make us better than our kind can bear,
Have dashed a spice of envy in the laws,
And straining up too high have spoiled the cause.
Yet some wise nations break their cruel chains,
And own no laws but those which love ordains;
Where happy daughters with their sires are joined,       60
And piety is doubly paid in kind.
O that I had been born in such a clime,
Not here, where 'tis the country makes the crime!
    But whither would my impious fancy stray?
Hence hopes, and ye forbidden thoughts away!
His worth deserves to kindle my desires,

But with the love that daughters bear to sires.
Then had not Cinyras my father been,
What hindered Myrrha's hopes to be his queen?
But the perverseness of my fate is such,                    70
That he's not mine because he's mine too much:
Our kindred-blood debars a better tie;
He might be nearer were he not so nigh.
Eyes and their objects never must unite:
Some distance is required to help the sight.
   Fain would I travel to some foreign shore,
Never to see my native country more,
So might I to myself myself restore;
So might my mind these impious thoughts remove,
And ceasing to behold, might cease to love.                 80
But stay I must, to feed my famished sight,
To talk, to kiss, and more, if more I might:
More, impious maid? What more canst thou design?
To make a monstrous mixture in thy line,
And break all statutes human and divine?
Canst thou be called, to save thy wretched life,
Thy mother's rival and thy father's wife?
Confound so many sacred names in one:
Thy brother's mother, sister to thy son!
And fear'st thou not to see th' infernal bands,             90
Their hands with snakes, with torches armed their hands,
Full at thy face th' avenging brands to bear,
And shake the serpents from their hissing hair?
But thou in time th' increasing ill control,
Nor first debauch the body by the soul;
Secure the sacred quiet of thy mind,
And keep the sanctions Nature has designed.'

# from **The First Book of Homer's Ilias**

## (1)

*Achilles, the bravest Greek warrior at the siege of Troy, is affronted by
King Agamemnon's declaration that he will seize Briseis, Achilles'
captive maiden, by force.*

At this th' impatient hero sourly smiled;
His heart impetuous in his bosom boiled,
And jostled by two tides of equal sway,
Stood for a while suspended in his way,
Betwixt his reason and his rage untamed;
One whispered soft, and one aloud reclaimed;
That only counselled to the safer side,                          290
This to the sword his ready hand applied.
Unpunished to support th' affront was hard,
Nor easy was th' attempt to force the guard;
But soon the thirst of vengeance fired his blood,
Half shone his falchion, and half sheathed it stood.
   In that nice moment, Pallas from above,
Commissioned by th' imperial wife of Jove,
Descended swift (the white-armed queen was loath
The fight should follow, for she favoured both).
Just as in act he stood, in clouds enshrined,                   300
Her hand she fastened on his hair behind;
Then backward by his yellow curls she drew,
To him, and him alone, confessed in view.
Tamed by superior force, he turned his eyes,
Aghast at first, and stupid with surprise;
But by her sparkling eyes and ardent look,
The virgin warrior known, he thus bespoke:
'Com'st thou, celestial, to behold my wrongs?
Then view the vengeance which to crimes belongs!'
   Thus he; the blue-eyed goddess thus rejoined:       310
'I come to calm thy turbulence of mind,
If reason will resume her sovereign sway,
And, sent by Juno, her commands obey.
Equal she loves you both, and I protect;

Then give thy guardian gods their due respect,
And cease contention. Be thy words severe,
Sharp as he merits, but the sword forbear.
An hour unhoped already wings her way,
When he his dire affront shall dearly pay;
When the proud King shall sue with treble gain,     320
To quit thy loss and conquer thy disdain.
But thou, secure of my unfailing word,
Compose thy swelling soul, and sheathe the sword.'
    The youth thus answered mild: 'Auspicious maid,
Heaven's will be mine and your commands obeyed.
The gods are just, and when, subduing sense,
We serve their powers, provide the recompense.'
IIe said, with surly faith believed her word,
And in the sheath, reluctant, plunged the sword.
Her message done, she mounts the blessed abodes,     330
And mixed among the Senate of the gods.
    At her departure his disdain returned;
The fire she fanned with greater fury burned,
Rumbling within till thus it found a vent:
    'Dastard and drunkard, mean and insolent,
Tongue-valiant hero, vaunter of thy might,
In threats the foremost, but the lag in fight;
When didst thou thrust amid the mingled press,
Content to bid the war aloof in peace?
Arms are the trade of each plebeian soul;     340
'Tis death to fight, but kingly to control.
Lordlike at ease, with arbitrary power,
To peel the chiefs, the people to devour;
These, traitor, are thy talents; safer far
Than to contend in fields and toils of war.
Nor couldst thou thus have dared the common hate,
Were not their souls as abject as their state.
But by this sceptre solemnly I swear –
Which never more green leaf or growing branch shall bear,
Torn from the tree and giv'n by Jove to those     350
Who laws dispense and mighty wrongs oppose –
That when the Grecians want my wonted aid,
No gift shall bribe it, and no prayer persuade.
When Hector comes, the homicide, to wield

His conquering arms, with corpse to strew the field;
Then shalt thou mourn thy pride, and late confess
My wrong repented when 'tis past redress.'
   He said, and with disdain in open view,
Against the ground his golden sceptre threw.

## (2)

*On Olympus, Juno is jealous of Jove's* tête-à-tête *with Thetis about her son Achilles' grievances.*

He moves into his hall; the powers resort,
Each from his house to fill the Sovereign's court;
Nor waiting summons nor expecting stood,
But met with reverence and received the god.
He mounts the throne, and Juno took her place,
But sullen discontent sate lowering on her face.    720
With jealous eyes at distance she had seen,
Whispering with Jove, the silver-footed queen;
Then, impotent of tongue, her silence broke,
Thus turbulent, in rattling tone, she spoke:
   'Author of ills, and close contriver Jove,
Which of thy dames, what prostitute of love,
Has held thy ear so long and begged so hard
For some old service done, some new reward?
Apart you talked, for that's your special care;
The consort never must the council share.    730
One gracious word is for a wife too much;
Such is a marriage vow, and Jove's own faith is such!'
   Then thus the sire of gods and men below:
'What I have hidden, hope not thou to know.
E'en goddesses are women; and no wife
Has power to regulate her husband's life.
Counsel she may, and I will give thy ear
The knowledge first of what is fit to hear.
What I transact with others or alone,
Beware to learn, nor press too near the throne.'    740
   To whom the goddess with the charming eyes:
'What hast thou said, O tyrant of the skies?

When did I search the secrets of thy reign,
Though privileged to know, but privileged in vain?
But well thou dost to hide from common sight
Thy close intrigues, too bad to bear the light.
Nor doubt I but the silver-footed dame,
Tripping from sea, on such an errand came,
To grace her issue at the Grecians' cost,
And for one peevish man destroy an host.'                    750
    To whom the Thunderer made this stern reply:
'My household curse, my lawful plague, the spy
Of Jove's designs, his other squinting eye!
Why this vain prying, and for what avail?
Jove will be master still, and Juno fail.
Should thy suspicious thoughts divine aright,
Thou but becom'st more odious to my sight
For this attempt; uneasy life to me,
Still watched and importuned, but worse for thee!
Curb that impetuous tongue, before too late                 760
The gods behold, and tremble at thy fate,
Pitying, but daring not in thy defence
To lift a hand against omnipotence.'
    This heard, th' imperious Queen sate mute with fear,
Nor further durst incense the gloomy Thunderer:
Silence was in the court at this rebuke;
Nor could the gods abashed sustain their sovereign's look.
    The limping smith observed the saddened feast,
And hopping here and there, himself a jest,
Put in his word, that neither might offend,                  770
To Jove obsequious, yet his mother's friend.
    'What end in heaven will be of civil war,
If gods of pleasure will for mortals jar?
Such discord but disturbs our jovial feast;
One grain of bad embitters all the best.
Mother, though wise yourself, my counsel weigh;
'Tis much unsafe my sire to disobey;
Not only you provoke him to your cost,
But mirth is marred and the good cheer is lost.
Tempt not his heavy hand, for he has power                   780
To throw you headlong from his heavenly tower;
But one submissive word which you let fall,

Will make him in good humour with us all.'
   He said no more, but crowned a bowl unbid,
The laughing nectar overlooked the lid;
Then put it to her hand, and thus pursued:
   'This cursed quarrel be no more renewed;
Be, as becomes a wife, obedient still,
Though grieved, yet subject to her husband's will.
I would not see you beaten, yet, afraid                    790
Of Jove's superior force, I dare not aid.
Too well I know him, since that hapless hour
When I and all the gods employed our power
To break your bonds; me by the heel he drew,
And o'er heaven's battlements with fury threw.
All day I fell: my flight at morn begun,
And ended not but with the setting sun.
Pitched on my head, at length the Lemnian ground
Received my battered skull, the Sinthians healed my wound.'
   At Vulcan's homely mirth his mother smiled,          800
And, smiling, took the cup the clown had filled.
The reconciler bowl went round the board,
Which emptied, the rude skinker still restored.
Loud fits of laughter seized the guests, to see
The limping god so deft at his new ministry.
The feast continued till declining light;
They drank, they laughed, they loved, and then 'twas night.
Nor wanted tuneful harp nor vocal choir;
The Muses sung, Apollo touched the lyre.
Drunken at last, and drowsy they depart,                  810
Each to his house, adorned with laboured art
Of the lame architect. The thundering god,
Ev'n he withdrew to rest, and had his load;
His swimming head to needful sleep applied,
And Juno lay unheeded by his side.

# *from* **The Cock and the Fox,**
# **or The Tale of the Nun's Priest, from Chaucer**

## (1)

*Chanticleer, a farmyard cock, enjoys rare bliss with his wife, Partlet.*

This gentle cock for solace of his life
Six misses had beside his lawful wife;
Scandal that spares no king, though ne'er so good,
Says they were all of his own flesh and blood;
His sisters both by sire and mother's side:
And sure their likeness showed them near allied.           60
But make the worst, the monarch did no more
Than all the Ptolemies had done before:
When incest is for interest of a nation,
'Tis made no sin by holy dispensation.
Some lines have been maintained by this alone,
Which by their common ugliness are known.
   But passing this as from our tale apart,
Dame Partlet was the sov'reign of his heart:
Ardent in love, outrageous in his play,
He feathered her a hundred times a day;           70
And she, that was not only passing fair,
But was withal discreet and debonair,
Resolved the passive doctrine to fulfil,
Though loath, and let him work his wicked will:
At board and bed was affable and kind,
According as their marriage vow did bind,
And as the church's precept had enjoined;
Ev'n since she was a sennight old, they say,
Was chaste and humble to her dying day,
Nor chick nor hen was known to disobey.           80
   By this her husband's heart she did obtain:
What cannot beauty joined with virtue gain?
She was his only joy and he her pride;
She, when he walked, went pecking by his side;
If spurning up the ground he sprung a corn,

The tribute in his bill to her was borne.
But oh what joy it was to hear him sing
In summer, when the day began to spring,
Stretching his neck and warbling in his throat,
Solus cum sola then was all his note.                              90
For in the days of yore the birds of parts
Were bred to speak, and sing, and learn the liberal arts.


### (2)

*Chanticleer has had a disturbing dream foretelling a disaster in the
farmyard, but thoughts of Partlet soon make him forget his troubles.*

Now roaming in the yard he spurned the ground,
And gave to Partlet the first grain he found,
Then often feathered her with wanton play,
And trod her twenty times ere prime of day,
And took by turns and gave so much delight,
Her sisters pined with envy at the sight.                          440
    He chucked again, when other corns he found,
And scarcely deigned to set a foot to ground,
But swaggered like a lord about his hall,
And his sev'n wives came running at his call . . .
Then turning, said to Partlet, 'See, my dear,
How lavish Nature has adorned the year,
How the pale primrose and blue violets spring,
And birds essay their throats disused to sing.
All these are ours, and I with pleasure see
Man strutting on two legs and aping me!                            460
An unfledged creature of a lumpish frame,
Indued with fewer particles of flame.
Our dame sits cowering o'er a kitchen fire,
I draw fresh air and Nature's works admire,
And ev'n this day in more delight abound
Than since I was an egg I ever found.'

## (3)

*The narrator speculates on whether Chanticleer's impending abduction*
*by Reynard the fox was predestined.*

O Chanticleer, in an unhappy hour
Didst thou forsake the safety of thy bower:
Better for thee thou hadst believed thy dream,
And not that day descended from the beam!
　But here the doctors eagerly dispute;
Some hold predestination absolute;
Some clerks maintain that heaven at first foresees,
And in the virtue of foresight decrees. 510
If this be so, then prescience binds the will,
And mortals are not free to good or ill;
For what he first foresaw, he must ordain,
Or its eternal prescience may be vain;
As bad for us as prescience had not been;
For, first or last, he's author of the sin:
And who says that, let the blaspheming man
Say worse ev'n of the devil if he can.
For how can that eternal power be just
To punish man, who sins because he must? 520
Or how can he reward a virtuous deed,
Which is not done by us, but first decreed?
　I cannot bolt this matter to the bran,
As Bradwardine and holy Austin can:
If prescience can determine actions so
That we must do, because he did foreknow,
Or that foreknowing, yet our choice is free,
Not forced to sin by strict necessity;
This strict necessity they simple call,
Another sort there is conditional. 530
The first so binds the will, that things foreknown
By spontaneity not choice are done.
Thus galley-slaves tug willing at their oar,
Consent to work, in prospect of the shore;
But would not work at all if not constrained before.
That other does not liberty constrain,
But man may either act or may refrain.

Heaven made us agents free to good or ill,
And forced it not, though he foresaw the will.
Freedom was first bestowed on human race,                    540
And prescience only held the second place.
    If he could make such agents wholly free,
I not dispute; the point's too high for me:
For heaven's unfathomed power what man can sound,
Or put to his omnipotence a bound?
He made us to his image all agree;
That image is the soul, and that must be
Or not the maker's image, or be free.
But whether it were better man had been
By nature bound to good, not free to sin,                     550
I waive, for fear of splitting on a rock:
The tale I tell is only of a cock.


# from **Ceyx and Alcyone**

## (1)

*Alcyone, Queen of Trachis, begs her husband not to undertake a sea
voyage. Her forebodings are justified when his ship encounters a
storm.*

Now waves on waves ascending scale the skies,
And in the fires above the water fries;
When yellow sands are sifted from below,
The glittering billows give a golden show;
And when the fouler bottom spews the black,
The Stygian dye the tainted waters take;                      130
Then frothy white appear the flatted seas,
And change their colour, changing their disease.
Like various fits the Trachin vessel finds,
And now sublime she rides upon the winds;
As from a lofty summit looks from high,
And from the clouds beholds the nether sky;
Now from the depth of hell they lift their sight,

And at a distance see superior light;
The lashing billows make a loud report,
And beat her sides, as battering rams a fort;                    140
Or as a lion, bounding in his way,
With force augmented bears against his prey,
Sidelong to seize, or unappalled with fear,
Springs on the toils and rushes on the spear;
So seas impelled by winds with added power
Assault the sides and o'er the hatches tower.
    The planks, their pitchy coverings washed away,
Now yield, and now a yawning breach display;
The roaring waters with a hostile tide
Rush through the ruins of her gaping side.                       150
Meantime in sheets of rain the sky descends,
And ocean, swelled with waters, upwards tends,
One rising, falling one; the heavens and sea
Meet at their confines in the middle way;
The sails are drunk with showers and drop with rain,
Sweet waters mingle with the briny main.
No star appears to lend his friendly light;
Darkness and tempest make a double night;
But flashing fires disclose the deep by turns,
And while the lightnings blaze, the water burns.                 160
    Now all the waves their scattered force unite;
And as a soldier, foremost in the fight,
Makes way for others and, an host alone,
Still presses on and urging gains the town;
So while th' invading billows come abreast,
The hero tenth advanced before the rest,
Sweeps all before him with impetuous sway,
And from the walls descends upon the prey;
Part following enter, part remain without,
With envy hear their fellows' conquering shout,                  170
And mount on others' backs, in hope to share
The city, thus become the seat of war.
    An universal cry resounds aloud,
The sailors run in heaps, a helpless crowd;
Art fails, and courage falls, no succour near;
As many waves, as many deaths appear.
One weeps, and yet despairs of late relief;

One cannot weep, his fears congeal his grief,
But stupid, with dry eyes expects his fate.
One with loud shrieks laments his lost estate,                    180
And calls those happy whom their funerals wait.
This wretch with prayers and vows the gods implores,
And ev'n the skies he cannot see adores.
That other on his friends his thoughts bestows,
His careful father and his faithful spouse.
The covetous worldling in his anxious mind
Thinks only on the wealth he left behind.
    All Ceyx his Alcyone employs,
For her he grieves, yet in her absence joys:
His wife he wishes and would still be near,                    190
Not her with him, but wishes him with her:
Now with last looks he seeks his native shore,
Which Fate has destined him to see no more;
He sought, but in the dark tempestuous night
He knew not whither to direct his sight.
So whirl the seas, such darkness blinds the sky,
That the black night receives a deeper dye.
    The giddy ship ran round; the tempest tore
Her mast, and overboard the rudder bore.
One billow mounts, and with a scornful brow,                    200
Proud of her conquest gained, insults the waves below;
Nor lighter falls than if some giant tore
Pindus and Athos with the freight they bore,
And tossed on seas; pressed with the ponderous blow,
Down sinks the ship within th' abyss below;
Down with the vessel sink into the main
The many, never more to rise again.
Some few on scattered planks with fruitless care
Lay hold and swim, but while they swim despair.


### (2)


*Iris visits the Cave of Sleep and asks the God of Sleep to send a dream
to Alcyone, informing her of her husband's fate.*


Near the Cimmerians, in his dark abode,

Deep in a cavern dwells the drowsy god;
Whose gloomy mansion nor the rising sun         270
Nor setting visits, nor the lightsome noon;
But lazy vapours round the region fly,
Perpetual twilight and a doubtful sky;
No crowing cock does there his wings display,
Nor with his horny bill provoke the day;
Nor watchful dogs, nor the more wakeful geese
Disturb with nightly noise the sacred peace;
Nor beast of nature, nor the tame are nigh,
Nor trees with tempests rocked, nor human cry;
But safe repose, without an air of breath        280
Dwells here, and a dumb quiet next to death.
   An arm of Lethe with a gentle flow,
Arising upwards from the rock below,
The palace moats, and o'er the pebbles creeps,
And with soft murmurs calls the coming sleeps;
Around its entry nodding poppies grow,
And all cool simples that sweet rest bestow;
Night from the plants their sleepy virtue drains,
And passing sheds it on the silent plains:
No door there was th' unguarded house to keep,     290
On creaking hinges turned to break his sleep.
   But in the gloomy court was raised a bed,
Stuffed with black plumes, and on an ebon stead;
Black was the covering too, where lay the god,
And slept supine, his limbs displayed abroad;
About his head fantastic visions fly,
Which various images of things supply,
And mock their forms: the leaves on trees not more,
Nor bearded ears in fields, nor sands upon the shore.

# from **The Wife of Bath her Tale**

*A young knight, found guilty of rape, has consented to marry an old crone, who, on their wedding night, delivers him a curtain-lecture on the nature of true and false nobility.*

'Know this, my lord: nobility of blood
Is but a glittering and fallacious good;
The nobleman is he whose noble mind
Is filled with inborn worth, unborrowed from his kind.
The King of Heaven was in a manger laid,
And took his earth but from an humble maid:
Then what can birth or mortal men bestow,
Since floods no higher than their fountains flow?
We who for name and empty honour strive,                     390
Our true nobility from him derive.
Your ancestors who puff your mind with pride,
And vast estates to mighty titles tied,
Did not your honour but their own advance;
For virtue comes not by inheritance.
If you tralineate from your father's mind,
What are you else but of a bastard kind?
Do as your great progenitors have done,
And by their virtues prove yourself their son.
No father can infuse or wit or grace;                        400
A mother comes across and mars the race.
A grandsire or a grandame taints the blood;
And seldom three descents continue good.
Were virtue by descent, a noble name
Could never villainize his father's fame;
But as the first, the last of all the line
Would like the sun ev'n in descending shine.
Take fire, and bear it to the darkest house,
Betwixt King Arthur's court and Caucasus,
If you depart, the flame shall still remain,                 410
And the bright blaze enlighten all the plain;
Nor till the fuel perish can decay,
By Nature formed on things combustible to prey.
Such is not man, who, mixing better seed

With worse begets a base, degenerate breed.
The bad corrupts the good, and leaves behind
No trace of all the great begetter's mind.
The father sinks within his son, we see,
And often rises in the third degree;
If better luck a better mother give,                                    420
Chance gave us being and by chance we live.
Such as our atoms were, ev'n such are we,
Or call it chance, or strong necessity:
Thus, loaded with dead weight, the will is free.
And thus it needs must be: for seed conjoined
Lets into Nature's work th' imperfect kind;
But fire, th' enlivener of the general frame,
Is one, its operation still the same.
Its principle is in itself: while ours
Works, as confederates war, with mingled powers;                       430
Or man or woman, whichsoever fails;
And oft the vigour of the worse prevails.
Ether with sulphur blended alters hue,
And casts a dusky gleam of Sodom blue.
Thus in a brute their ancient honour ends,
And the fair mermaid in a fish descends:
The line is gone; no longer duke or earl
But, by himself degraded, turns a churl.
Nobility of blood is but renown
Of thy great fathers by their virtue known,                            440
And a long trail of light to thee descending down.
If in thy smoke it ends, their glories shine;
But infamy and villainage are thine.
Then what I said before is plainly showed,
That true nobility proceeds from God:
Not left us by inheritance, but given
By bounty of our stars and grace of heaven.'

# from Of the Pythagorean Philosophy, from Ovid's *Metamorphoses*, Book Fifteen

## (1)

*The Greek philosopher Pythagoras discourses on the immortality of the soul.*

'Now since the god inspires me to proceed,
Be that whate'er inspiring power obeyed;
For I will sing of mighty mysteries,                          210
Of truths concealed before from human eyes,
Dark oracles unveil, and open all the skies.
Pleased as I am to walk along the sphere
Of shining stars, and travel with the year,
To leave the heavy earth, and scale the height
Of Atlas, who supports the heavenly weight;
To look from upper light, and thence survey
Mistaken mortals wandering from the way
And wanting wisdom, fearful for the state
Of future things, and trembling at their fate!               220
    Those I would teach, and by right reason bring .
To think of death as but an idle thing,
Why thus affrighted at an empty name,
A dream of darkness and fictitious flame?
Vain themes of wit which but in poems pass,
And fables of a world that never was!
What feels the body when the soul expires,
By time corrupted, or consumed by fires?
Nor dies the spirit, but new life repeats
In other forms, and only changes seats . . .                 230
    Then death, so called, is but old matter dressed
In some new figure, and a varied vest;
Thus all things are but altered, nothing dies,
And here and there th' unbodied spirit flies,                240
By time or force or sickness dispossessed,
And lodges where it lights in man or beast;
Or hunts without, till ready limbs it find,

And actuates those according to their kind;
From tenement to tenement is tossed;
The soul is still the same, the figure only lost:
And as the softened wax new seals receives,
This face assumes, and that impression leaves;
Now called by one, now by another name,
The form is only changed, the wax is still the same:          250
So death, so called, can but the form deface;
Th' immortal soul flies out in empty space,
To seek her fortune in some other place.'

## (2)

*Pythagoras describes the perpetual flux of nature.*

'And since, like Tiphys parting from the shore,          260
In ample seas I sail, and depths untried before,
This let me further add, that Nature knows
No steadfast station, but or ebbs or flows;
Ever in motion, she destroys her old,
And casts new figures in another mould.
Ev'n times are in perpetual flux, and run
Like rivers from their fountain rolling on;
For time no more than streams is at a stay;
The flying hour is ever on her way;
And as the fountain still supplies her store,          270
The wave behind impels the wave before.
   Thus in successive course the minutes run,
And urge their predecessor minutes on,
Still moving, ever new; for former things
Are set aside like abdicated kings,
And every moment alters what is done,
And innovates some act till then unknown.'

## (3)

*Pythagoras describes the ages of man.*

'Time was when we were sowed, and just began
From some few fruitful drops, the promise of a man;

Then Nature's hand, fermented as it was,
Moulded to shape the soft, coagulated mass,
And when the little man was fully formed,
The breathless embryo with a spirit warmed;
But when the mother's throes begin to come,                    330
The creature, pent within the narrow room,
Breaks his blind prison, pushing to repair
His stifled breath and draw the living air;
Cast on the margin of the world he lies,
A helpless babe, but by instinct he cries.
He next essays to walk, but downward pressed
On four feet imitates his brother beast:
By slow degrees he gathers from the ground
His legs, and to the rolling chair is bound;
Then walks alone; a horseman now become,                      340
He rides a stick and travels round the room:
In time he vaunts among his youthful peers,
Strong-boned and strung with nerves, in pride of years:
He runs with mettle his first merry stage,
Maintains the next abated of his rage,
But manages his strength and spares his age.
Heavy the third and stiff, he sinks apace,
And though 'tis down-hill all, but creeps along the race.
Now sapless on the verge of death he stands,
Contemplating his former feet and hands;                      350
And Milo-like his slackened sinews sees
And withered arms, once fit to cope with Hercules,
Unable now to shake, much less to tear the trees.'

# The Secular Masque

*Enter Janus*

JANUS          Chronos, Chronos, mend thy pace,
An hundred times the rolling sun
Around the radiant belt has run
In his revolving race.
Behold, behold, the goal in sight,
Spread thy fans, and wing thy flight.

*Enter Chronos, with a scythe in his hand and a great
globe on his back, which he sets down at his entrance*

CHRONOS     Weary, weary of my weight,
Let me, let me drop my freight,
    And leave the world behind.
I could not bear                   10
Another year
The load of human kind.

*Enter Momus, laughing*

MOMUS       Ha! ha! ha! ha! ha! ha! well hast thou done,
    To lay down thy pack,
    And lighten thy back.
The world was a fool e'er since it begun,
And since neither Janus, nor Chronos, nor I
    Can hinder the crimes,
    Or mend the bad times,
'Tis better to laugh than to cry.          20
CHORUS OF ALL THREE   *'Tis better to laugh than to cry.*
JANUS          Since Momus comes to laugh below.
    Old Time begin the show,
That he may see in every scene,
What changes in this age have been,
CHRONOS     Then, Goddess of the silver bow, begin.

*Horns, or hunting-music within*

*Enter Diana*

DIANA    With horns and with hounds I waken the day,
       And hie to my woodland walks away;
       I tuck up my robe and am buskined soon,
       And tie to my forehead a waxing moon.   30
       I course the fleet stag, unkennel the fox,
       And chase the wild goats o'er summits of rocks,
       With shouting and hooting we pierce through the
         sky;
       And Echo turns hunter and doubles the cry.

CHORUS OF ALL *With shouting and hooting we pierce through the sky;*
       *And Echo turns hunter and doubles the cry.*

JANUS     Then our age was in its prime,
CHRONOS   Free from rage,
DIANA         —and free from crime,
MOMUS    A very merry, dancing, drinking,
       Laughing, quaffing, and unthinking time.  40

CHORUS OF ALL *Then our age was in its prime,*
       *Free from rage, and free from crime,*
       *A very merry, dancing, drinking,*
       *Laughing, quaffing, and unthinking time.*

*Dance of Diana's attendants*

*Enter Mars*

MARS      Inspire the vocal brass, inspire;
       The world is past its infant age:
         Arms and honour,
         Arms and honour,
       Set the martial mind on fire,
       And kindle manly rage.       50
       Mars has looked the sky to red;
       And peace, the lazy good, is fled.
       Plenty, peace and pleasure fly;
         The sprightly green
       In woodland-walks no more is seen;
       The sprightly green has drunk the Tyrian dye.

CHORUS OF ALL *Plenty, peace and pleasure fly;*
       *The sprightly green*
       *In woodland-walks no more is seen;*

|   |   |   |
|---|---|---|
| | *The sprightly green has drunk the Tyrian dye.* | 60 |
| MARS | Sound the trumpet, beat the drum, | |
| | Through all the world around; | |
| | Sound a reveille, sound, sound, | |
| | The warrior god is come. | |

CHORUS OF ALL  *Sound the trumpet, beat the drum,*
          *Through all the world around;*
          *Sound a reveille, sound, sound,*
            *The warrior god is come.*

MOMUS     Thy sword within the scabbard keep,
          And let mankind agree;            70
          Better the world were fast asleep
            Than kept awake by thee.
          The fools are only thinner
            With all our cost and care;
          But neither side a winner,
            For things are as they were.

CHORUS OF ALL  *The fools are only thinner*
            *With all our cost and care;*
          *But neither side a winner,*
            *For things are as they were.*    80


*Enter Venus*

VENUS      Calms appear when storms are past;
          Love will have his hour at last:
          Nature is my kindly care;
          Mars destroys and I repair;
          Take me, take me, while you may,
          Venus comes not every day.

CHORUS OF ALL  *Take her, take her, while you may,*
           *Venus comes not every day.*

CHRONOS  The world was then so light,
          I scarcely felt the weight;       90
          Joy ruled the day, and Love the night.
          But since the Queen of Pleasure left the ground,
            I faint, I lag,
             And feebly drag
          The ponderous orb around.

MOMUS     All, all of a piece throughout;
          [*pointing to Diana*]

Thy chase had a beast in view;
[*to Mars*]
Thy wars brought nothing about;
[*to Venus*]
Thy lovers were all untrue.

JANUS                   'Tis well an old age is out,                    100
CHRONOS             And time to begin a new.
CHORUS OF ALL    *All, all of a piece throughout;*
                            *Thy chase had a beast in view;*
                            *Thy wars brought nothing about;*
                            *Thy lovers were all untrue.*
                            *'Tis well an old age is out,*
                            *And time to begin a new.*

                            *Dance of huntsmen, nymphs, warriors, and lovers.*

# Notes

**from _Annus Mirabilis_** Published 1667. The poem depicts the events of the Dutch War of 1665–6. **(1) 505 Prince:** Prince Rupert, joint-commander of the English fleet in the Four Days Battle (1–4 June 1666). **508 home:** precisely on his target. **512 heartless:** dispirited. **518 by the board:** overboard. **520 offends:** attacks. **526 flix:** fur. **(2) 718 ambushed:** lurking. **(3)** The Fire (2–5 September 1666) destroyed two-thirds of the City of London, including St Paul's Cathedral. **885 letted of:** hindered from attaining.

**from _Marriage A-la-Mode_** Published 1673.

**from _Aureng-Zebe_** Published 1676. **7 cozenage:** fraud. **11 chemic:** made by alchemy.

**from _Mac Flecknoe_** Circulated in MS, 1676. Published (unauthorized) 1682, (authorized) 1684. The poem depicts, in mock-heroic style, the coronation of Dryden's critical adversary, the minor dramatist Thomas Shadwell, as Monarch of Dullness, in succession to the hack writer Richard Flecknoe: both had, hubristically, claimed to be literary heirs of Ben Jonson. **26 Thoughtless:** (i) without thought; (ii) carefree. **27 supinely:** face-upwards, lazily.

**from _Absalom and Achitophel_** Published 1681. The poem treats, in the form of a biblical allegory (based on Absalom's rebellion against King David in 2 Samuel), the events of the Popish Plot and Exclusion Crisis of 1678–81 (see Chronology). **(1) 7 Israel's monarch:** King David (= Charles II). **11 Michal:** Catherine of Braganza, the Portuguese princess whom Charles II married in 1662; she had no children. **13–14:** Charles II had fourteen acknowledged illegitimate children. **18 Absalon:** James Scott, Duke of Monmouth (1649–85), son of Charles II and Lucy Walter. The variant spelling is adopted for the rhyme. **20 gust:** relish. **23–4:** Monmouth had served with distinction against the Dutch, French and Scots in the 1660s and 1670s. **(2) 150 Achitophel:** Anthony Ashley Cooper (1621–83), leader of the exclusionist opposition, and, in Dryden's poem, the evil genius prompting Absalom to rebel against his father. Shaftesbury was small of stature and suffered from a troublesome wound in the side, the result of an operation for a cyst on the liver. **152 close:** secret. **158 o'erinformed:** filled to excess, over-animated. **171 huddled:** concealed, confused. **(3) 544 Zimri:** George Villiers, Duke of Buckingham (1628–87), prominent among the opposition leaders in the later 1670s. Villiers dabbled in chemistry, was an accomplished violinist and lost a vast fortune by profligate spending. **552 freaks:** whims. **559 peculiar:** particular, special.

**from *The Second Part of Absalom and Achitophel*** Published 1682. **458 tun:** cask. **459 Og:** Shadwell (see under *Mac Flecknoe*, above), known for his Whiggish sympathies, opium addiction and drunkenness. The biblical King Og (Deuteronomy 3, 1–11) was renowned for his bulk. **461 link:** torch. **480 make:** constitution. **481 nativity:** horoscope.

**from *Religio Laici*** Published 1682. The poem is a 'layman's' defence of Anglicanism against the arguments of Deists, Catholics and Dissenters. **(1) 4 discover:** reveal. **21 the Stagyrite:** Aristotle (born at Stagira), who held that the universe is directed by an 'unmoved mover'. **22 Epicurus:** Greek philosopher (341–270 BC), who held that the universe is composed of atoms, colliding and combining in a void.

**To the *Memory of Mr Oldham*** Published 1684. John Oldham was a promising young poet who had died in 1683. His satires were renowned for their 'rough' versification. **9 Nisus:** In Book V of Virgil's *Aeneid*, Nisus is on the point of winning a foot-race when he slips and falls; he trips the next runner, thereby allowing his younger friend, Euryalus, to win. **14 numbers:** versification. **20 quickness:** sharpness, pungency. **23 Marcellus:** the nephew and adoptive son of Augustus, who was expected to succeed him as Roman emperor, but who died prematurely in 23 BC.

**from *Sylvae, or The Second Part of Poetical Miscellanies*** Published 1685.

**from *Lucretius: The Beginning of the First Book*** Lucretius' *De Rerum Natura* ('On the Nature of Things') is a poem on the nature of the physical world, based on the philosophy of Epicurus (see above, under *Religio Laici*). **2 Parent of Rome:** Venus, the mother of Aeneas, and thus of the Roman people. **17 genial:** leading to propagation. **19 tempt:** venture on. **46 thy dreadful servant:** Mars, Venus' lover. **54 involved:** enmeshed.

**from *Translation of the Latter Part of the Third Book of Lucretius: Against the Fear of Death* (1) 4 Punic:** Carthaginian (a reference to the 'Punic' wars between Carthage and Rome in the 1st century BC). **(3) 185 Tantalus:** mythological king, punished by the gods by having a rock suspended above him which prevented him from eating or drinking. **189 Tityus:** mythological giant, punished for his attempted rape of the goddess Leto by having his liver perpetually torn by two vultures. **200 Sisyphus:** a legendary king of Corinth, condemned eternally to push a large stone to the top of a hill. **206 still:** always. **211 smokes:** raises dust. **(4) 276 vow:** devote themselves to.

**from *Lucretius: The Fourth Book, Concerning the Nature of Love* 42 unsincere:** not unmixed, not unalloyed. **52 still:** increasingly. **56 repletion:** satisfaction. **62 fleet:** fly swiftly. **69 strain:** embrace tightly. **80 momentany:** lasting only a moment. **84 nerves:** muscles, tendons. **86 recruited:** replenished.

***Horace: Book 1, Ode 9* 32 pointed:** fixed.

***Horace: Book 3, Ode 29, Paraphrased in Pindaric Verse*** Horace's Ode is addressed to his patron, Maecenas, whose residence had a panoramic view of Rome. **2 Tuscan:** Maecenas was from an aristocratic Etruscan family. **3 generous:** strong. **6 artful:** skilful. **23 vicissitude:** change. **fit:** short spell. **24 treat:** feast. **27 Tyrian:** purple (the colour of rich room hangings). **30 The Sirian star:** the 'dog star', whose influence supposedly created great heat. **33 fry:** get very hot. **37 sylvans:** countrymen. **39 want:** need. **42 Gallic:** Horace refers to the east: Dryden's readers would think of Louis XIV. **43 quiver-bearing foe:** the Parthians (enemies of Rome, and renowned archers). **64 honours:** leaves. **75 office:** employment. **96 main:** ocean. **99 pinnace:** small boat.

***A New Song* 4 tousing:** pulling, tugging. **14 Trimmer:** political opportunist who changes sides according to which party is in the ascendant.

**from *To the Pious Memory of . . . Mrs Anne Killigrew*** Published 1685, in Anne Killigrew's *Poems* (dated 1686). Anne Killigrew, a talented poet and painter, had died of smallpox in 1685, aged twenty-five. **Title Mrs:** Miss. **2 promotion:** exaltation to sainthood. **6 neighbouring star:** planet closest to earth (as opposed to the 'fixed stars' of the larger planetary sphere). **12 space:** length of time. **16 rehearse:** relate, declare. **21 probationer:** novice. **22 candidate:** catechumen.

**from *The Hind and the Panther*** Published 1687. The poem is a defence of Roman Catholicism, in the form of a beast-fable in which 'a milk white hind' represents the Catholic church and a 'spotted panther' the Church of England. **262 prerogative:** royal privilege. **265 for:** because. **279 Cain:** eldest son of Adam and Eve, murderer of his younger brother, Abel. **283 the mighty hunter:** Nimrod (Genesis 10, 8–12).

***A Song for St Cecilia's Day, 1687*** Published 1687. Performed, with music by Giovanni Battista Draghi, at the annual celebrations in Stationers' Hall (22 November) of the feast of Cecilia, patron saint of music. **5 heave:** lift up. **9 stations:** positions **15 diapason:** octave (the most perfect harmony). **17 Jubal:** the father of all harpists and organists (Genesis 4, 21), said to have made a lute out of a tortoise shell. **47 mend:** improve. **48 Orpheus:** said to have charmed the beasts, trees and rocks with his music. **50 Sequacious of:** ready to follow. **60 This crumbling pageant:** (i) the universe; (ii) the assembled performers of the Ode on their makeshift scaffolding. **63 untune:** (by heralding the Last Judgement).

**from *Eleonora*** Published 1692, in memory of Eleonora, Countess of Abingdon.

**from *The Satires of Juvenal and Persius*** Published 1692 (dated 1693). The Roman satirist Juvenal was admired by Dryden for his hyperbolically splenetic wit: 'he gives me as much pleasure as I can bear; . . . When he gives over, 'tis a sign the subject is exhausted, and the wit of man can carry it no farther.'

**from *The Sixth Satire of Juvenal*** The satire concerns the vices of women. **168 cope with:** encounter. **188 bedight:** dressed.

**from *The Tenth Satire of Juvenal*** The satire depicts the futility of human longings for wealth, power, long life, old age and beauty. **(1) 99 Capitol:** the Capitoline Hill in Rome, site of the main temple of Jupiter. **109 noisy letter:** Tiberius, fearing that Sejanus was plotting against him, denounced him in a letter to the Senate. **112 Ethiop:** negroid. **135 dipped:** implicated. **139 spurn:** kick. **146 levees:** ceremonial morning visits to powerful men. **152–5:** Tiberius retired to Capri, where he was said to have indulged in debauchery and astrology. **159 want:** lack. **165:** mayors were responsible for the supervision of weights and measures. **(2) 307 ropy:** glutinous. **326 palled to:** unable to taste. **328 limber nerve:** penis.

**from _To my Dear Friend, Mr Congreve_** Published 1693 (dated 1694). William Congreve (1670–1729), poet, playwright and member of Dryden's circle, wrote a Dedication to the 1717 edition of Dryden's _Dramatic Works_. **41 my laurel:** the Poet Laureateship (see Chronology). **45 one Edward:** Edward II. **46 a greater Edward:** Edward III. **48 Tom the Second:** Thomas Rymer, made Historiographer Royal in 1692. **Tom the First:** Thomas Shadwell, made Poet Laureate and Historiographer Royal in 1689. **49 my patron:** the Earl of Dorset, who as Lord Chamberlain appointed the Laureate and Historiographer. **55 Thy first attempt:** Congreve's first play, _The Old Bachelor_ (1693). **56 this:** _The Double Dealer_. **58 regular:** observant of the dramatic Unities. **61 portion:** endowment.

**_Ode on the Death of Mr Henry Purcell_** Published 1696, together with a musical setting by John Blow. Henry Purcell, the greatest English composer of the seventeenth century, had died on 21 November 1695, aged thirty-six. **3 strain:** exert. **6 Philomel:** the nightingale. **10 crew:** (of musicians). **16 Opheus:** the poet-musician _par excellence_ of Greek myth. **18 their sovereigns':** Pluto and Proserpina, king and queen of the Underworld, charmed by Orpheus' singing. **31 mend:** correct.

**from _The Works of Virgil_** Published 1697, revised 1698 (texts in this edition are based on 1698).

**from _The Second Book of the Georgics_** Virgil's _Georgics_ presents a picture of Italian and rural life and the natural world, dealing, in turn, with agriculture and the cultivation of trees, the rearing of cattle and bee-keeping. **1 443 kindly:** generative. **455 gems:** buds. **461 tenour:** continuity. **(2) 703 sylvans:** wood gods. **710 descents:** attacks, invasions. **726 citron:** a fragrant wood. **727 Tyrian:** with purple coverings. **749 several:** single. **751 yeaning:** giving birth. **prevent:** anticipate. **755 mast:** fruit of the beech or oak. **773 butts:** archery targets.

**from _The Third Book of the Georgics_** **403 the youth:** Leander, who drowned swimming the Hellespont to visit Hero at Sestus. **424 their**

**master:** Glaucus, who was torn to pieces by his own mares for having offended Venus.

**from *The Fourth Book of the Georgics*** **92** **intestine:** internal. **94** **the vulgar:** the ordinary bees. **115** **shocking:** clashing.

**from *The Second Book of the Aeneis*** **702** **Doddered:** entwined with tendrils. **704** **Hecuba:** Priam's queen. **719** **Pyrrhus:** son of Achilles. **752** **pile:** altar, pyre. **753** **falchion:** crooked sword. **757** **distained:** stained.

**from *The Fourth Book of the Aeneis*** **(1)** **103** **Tyrian:** Dido had fled to Carthage from Tyre. **113** **depends:** hangs. **(2)** **258** **the Titanian birth:** Virgil imagines Fame as having been begotten by Earth in revenge for the Olympians' defeat of Earth's other children, the Titans. **273** **prodigies:** marvels, monstrous happenings. **(3)** **525** **Hyrcanian:** from Hyrcania, near the Caspian Sea. **534** **equal:** fair. **544** **Lycian lots:** oracles of Apollo. **(4)** **642** **mast:** acorns.

**from *The Eighth Book of the Aeneis*** An earlier version of this episode had appeared in *Sylvae* (1685) **509** **Phrygian:** Trojan. **521** **obnoxious:** susceptible.

**from *The Ninth Book of the Aeneis*** An earlier version of this episode had appeared in *Sylvae* (1685). **502** **Volscens:** a Latin chief. **503** **The Queen:** Amata, wife of King Latinus. **506** **doubtful:** murky, indistinct. **515** **belay:** enclose. **519** **Horrid:** bristling. **521** **prey:** the helmet of Messapus, looted by Euryalus. **522** **the younger:** Euryalus. **534** **coursers:** horses. **537** **Forelaid:** ambushed. **546** **Queen:** Diana, the moon goddess. **582** **share:** plough. **588** **bored:** pushed out of the way. **592** **weazon:** windpipe.

***Alexander's Feast, or the Power of Music: An Ode in Honour of St Cecilia's Day*** Published 1697, and performed at that year's St Cecilia's day celebrations (see under *A Song for St Cecilia's Day, 1687*). Alexander the Great was the son of Philip II of Macedon and Olympias. According to some legends he was the son of Jove, who had impregnated Olympias in the form of a serpent. Dryden's poem narrates events following Alexander's conquest of Persia and defeat of the Persian king, Darius II. The Greeks are feasting in

Persepolis (Darius' capital) and being entertained by Timotheus, Alexander's court musician. **3 awful:** awesome. **7 myrtles:** (sacred to Venus). **9 Thais:** Alexander's mistress. **29 spires:** wreaths, spirals. **47 Bacchus:** god of wine. **53 hautboys:** oboes. **69 The master:** Timotheus. **85 Revolving:** considering. **94 in the next degree:** only one key away. **97 Lydian measures:** (noted for their melancholy). **107 The many:** the audience. **147 flambeau:** flaming torch. **161 Cecilia:** patron saint of music. **162 vocal frame:** the organ.

**from** *Fables Ancient and Modern*  Published 1700.

**from** *Palamon and Arcite, or The Knight's Tale, from Chaucer*  From Book III. **1039 suborn:** procure. **1063 periods:** conclusions. **1074 Retchless:** heedless. **1076 vegetive:** able to grow. **1111 annoy:** trouble. **1112 vicissitude:** change of circumstance.

**from** *Sigismonda and Guiscardo, from Boccace*  Dryden translates Boccaccio, *Decameron* 4, 1. **410 election:** choice. **452 inured:** accustomed. **454 incontinence:** unchastity.

**from** *Baucis and Philemon, out of the Eighth Book of Ovid's Metamorphoses* **46 officious:** kind, busy. **54 chips:** small pieces of wood. **57 seether:** pot. **89 grateful:** pleasing.

**from** *Cinyras and Myrrha, out of the Tenth Book of Ovid's* Metamorphoses  **90 th' infernal bands:** the Furies.

**from** *The First Book of Homer's Ilias* (1) **297 nice:** exact. **305 stupid:** dumbfounded. **321 quit:** recompense. **343 peel:** steal from. (2) **718 the god:** Jove. **722 the silver-footed queen:** Thetis, Achilles' mother. **792 that hapless hour:** an occasion when Vulcan intervened in a quarrel between Jove and Juno and was thrown out of heaven for his pains; he landed on Lemnos and was healed by the Sintians. **803 skinker:** potman in an alehouse. **still:** constantly. **808 wanted:** was lacking.

**from** *The Cock and the Fox, or The Tale of the Nun's Priest, from Chaucer* (1) **56 misses:** mistresses. **61 make the worst:** however bad you think his conduct was. **62 Ptolemies:** Egyptian kings, some of whom married their sisters. **63–4:** Dryden alludes to Henry VIII's divorce from Catherine of Arragon. **65–6:** an allusion to the Habsburgs. **73 pas-**

**sive doctine:** the belief that to resist lawful authority is impious.
**78 sennight:** week. **85 spurning:** kicking. **90 Solus cum sola:** a
monkish proverb ('If a man is alone with a woman, you won't expect them
to be saying their prayers') used in the sixteenth century as the title for a
song. **90 all his note:** (i) the entire subject of his song; (ii) what he was
famous for. **91 birds of parts:** (i) talented birds; (ii) birds good at part-
singing. **(2) 438 prime of day:** dawn. **(3) 523 bolt:** sift. **524 Brad-
wardine:** Archbishop Thomas Bradwardine (?1290–1349), celebrated
theologian. **Austin:** St Augustine.

**from Ceyx and Alcyone** From Ovid, *Metamorphoses* XI. **(1) 130 Sty-
gian:** hellish. **144 toils:** nets. **203 Pindus and Athos:** celebrated
mountains. **(2) 268 Cimmerians:** legendary cave-dwellers in a remote
region. **275 provoke:** arouse. **282 Lethe:** the river of oblivion in Hades.
**287 simples:** drugs. **288 virtue:** medicinal effectiveness. **295 abroad:**
in all directions. **299 ears:** spikes of corn.

**from The Wife of Bath her Tale** **396 tralineate:** deviate. **428 still:**
always. **434 Sodom blue:** sulphurous blue (the colour of the flames
which burnt Sodom).

**from Of the Pythagorean Philosophy, from Ovid's Metamorphoses,
Book** XV **(1) 238 vest:** outer garment. **(2) 260 Tiphys:** helmsman of
the Argo. **265 figures:** shapes. **275 abdicated:** James II was said to have
'abdicated', thus leaving the throne 'vacant' for William III. **(3) 339 roll-
ing chair:** walking frame on wheels. **343 nerves:** muscles. **345 rage:**
eagerness of mind. **351 Milo:** Greek athlete and strong-man.

**The Secular Masque** Published 1700, as an addition to Sir John
Vanbrugh's revision of Fletcher's *The Pilgrim*. The masque surveys the
events of the seventeenth century, in the the form of a conversation
between Janus (the god of beginnings), Chronos (the god of time,
represented as carrying a scythe in his hand and the world on his back),
Momus (god of mockery and laughter), Diana (goddess of hunting) and
Mars (god of war). **Secular:** relating to the century (*saeculum* = century).
**6 fans:** wings. **56 Tyrian:** purple (i.e. blood-coloured).